LUCKY SPOOL'S
ESSENTIAL GUIDE
MODERN to
QUILT MAKING

Compiled by Susanne Woods

Published in 2014 by Lucky Spool Media, LLC
P.O. Box 270142, Louisville, CO 80027
www.luckyspool.com
info@luckyspool.com

TEXT © The Individual Designers
EDITOR Susanne Woods
ILLUSTRATIONS Kari Vojtechovsky
DESIGNERS Casey Dukes and Liz Quan

9 8 7 6 5 4 3 2 1
First Edition
Printed and bound in China
Library of Congress Cataloging-in-Publication
Data available upon request
ISBN 978-1-940655-00-0

LSID0010

Table of Contents

The Workshops

Introduction

Just like you, I am passionate about modern quilting. As a community that discovered one another online, we have quickly succeeded in creating ways to connect in person through regional Modern Quilt Guilds, QuiltCon, and a huge (and growing) number of local quilting retreats. We have demonstrated that we have a lasting passion for the craft and an insatiable desire to learn. While there are many online classes, tutorials, and blogs that are wonderful sources of inspiration and information, nothing rivals attending a workshop taught by an experienced teacher.

Within our modern quilting space, there are a handful of those teachers who have established themselves as the most in-demand instructors and teach regularly. With our busy lives, not everyone can carve out the time or manage the travel expenses necessary to attend their workshops or lectures. So, I invited ten of these talented instructors to share their most-requested class here with you in this book. I hope you try something new and as you go through each workshop with your friends, guilds or online groups, that you share what you make and learn from these classes to help enrich, excite, and inspire all of us who are passionate about modern.

How to Use This Book

Each of these workshops is designed to help the intermediate quilt maker learn new skills, explore new options, and expand their quilt making 'toolbox'. Because of this, you won't find Beginning Quilting instructions here. We listened to our readers and packed as much beyond-the-beginner information as we could into this printed book. If you are a beginner, never fear! Lucky Spool is dedicated to expanding the number of voices contributing to our shared quilt making history, and we are here to help you develop your voice. Please go to www.luckyspool.com for a free downloadable PDF containing all the basics you will need to know to make successful quilts.

I can't wait to see what you create!

PRINCIPLES OF COLOR

A DESIGN WORKSHOP

Goal of the class: Using color successfully is often a quilter's biggest challenge. This workshop will train you to see color with a more critical eye. By doing this, you will begin to immediately recognize why certain colors work together, making your own color usage more effective and intentional.

TEACHER:
Kari
Vojtechovsky

BREAKING IT DOWN

Any color can be thought of in three dimensions: hue, value, and saturation. Breaking down color by these three parameters is the foundation for understanding all color relationships. In order to apply to color theory in a quilt, I'll first explain what these these important terms mean so we can use them when going over specific concepts and techniques.

Hue

Hue is the location of a color in the color spectrum. It refers to only the pure color. Every hue has many variations, from light to dark and from intense to muted. For example, navy is a variation of the pure hue blue.

Even though all colors in this block are different, they all have nearly the same hue.

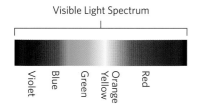

Visible Light Spectrum

Violet Blue Green Yellow Orange Red

Value

Value is the lightness or darkness of a color. It ranges from the purest white to the darkest black and everything in between. When evaluating value, think about where that color would be on a scale from light to dark.

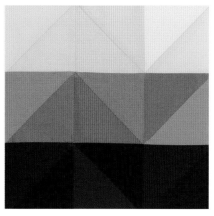

The row on the top has the lightest value and the row on the bottom has the darkest value.

Saturation

Saturation is the hue's degree of purity. It can be thought of as how vibrant or dull a color appears. A color with very high saturation is intense and a color with low saturation is muted. The more black, white, or gray a color has in its makeup, the less saturated it will be. The colors we call neutrals are actually very desaturated hues.

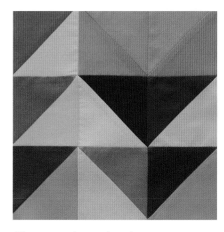

The row on the top has the most saturation and the row on the bottom has the least saturation.

IDENTIFYING DIFFERENT VALUE AND SATURATION OF A HUE

In any quilt, you will need to select a range of values for your design. You will also be choosing from various saturation levels. (Make sure to see the Working with Prints workshop on page 40. When designing his quilts, Dan identifies the values and saturation before he even looks at fabrics.) There are three ways to create colors of different value and saturation of a hue: by adding white, black, or gray to that hue. The technical terms for these colors are tints, shades, and tones, respectively.

These fabrics are as close as we can get to a pure hue with commercially available fabrics. They are highly saturated and have mostly mid-range value.

Tints: *A tint is a pure hue with added white. All tints will be lighter in value. The more white there is in the color, the lighter in value and less saturated it will be. Tints are light, pastel, and clear.*

Shades: *A shade is a pure hue with added black. All shades will be darker in value. The more black there is in the color, the darker in value and less saturated it will be. Shades are rich, dramatic, and dark.*

Tones: *A tone is a pure hue with added gray. A gray can be almost white or black, so a tone of can be nearly any value and saturation. It can have just a hint of a hue in it (like a gray that is a little blue), or it can be nearly as saturated as a pure hue. Tones are complex. They can be earthy, moody, and subtle.*

Putting It Together

The diagram to the right charts the interaction between the three aspects of a color—value, hue, and saturation—and how tints, shades, and tones take a hue from more to less saturated and from light to dark in value. Every color we see can be plotted out like this.

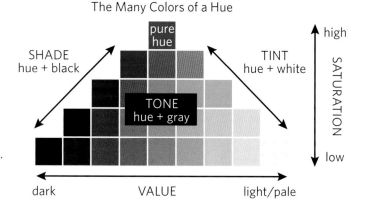

The Many Colors of a Hue

pure hue

SHADE
hue + black

TINT
hue + white

TONE
hue + gray

SATURATION

high

low

dark   VALUE   light/pale

Real-life Examples

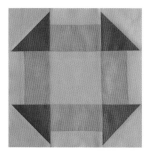 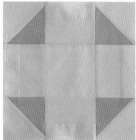 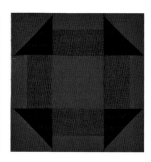

Let's practice recognizing these characteristics in real quilt blocks by comparing these Churn Dash blocks, above.

HUE: First, let's look at hue. Even though all of the colors are very different, each of these blocks uses the same hues in the same position. The background is tur-quoise, and the churn dash design is made of orange and red.

VALUE: Next, let's examine how value is used. Within each block, the value relationship is the same: orange is lightest, red is dark-est, and turquoise is in between; however, each complete block has a different overall value, with the lightest block in the middle and the darkest block on the right.

SATURATION: Finally, let's com-pare saturation levels. Within each block, the turquoise, orange and red are all similarly saturated. The block on the left has the highest saturation. The middle block is de-saturated by containing fabric col-ors that are tints. The block on the right is desaturated by containing fabric colors that are shades.

Now that you are familiar with the terminology, we can dive into using value, saturation, and hue to your advantage in your next quilt.

WORKING WITH VALUE

Value is an important color principle that any quilter needs to under-stand in order to make a successful quilt. Contrast defines the quilt design, and the primary way to create contrast is through value. Fabrics with the same value will blend together even if they have a different hue. If you find that your quilt design is muddled and lacking a clear focal point, it is often because there is not enough contrast in value. The quilt examples (right) can be made from the same number of half square triangles, but the value placement creates totally different designs.

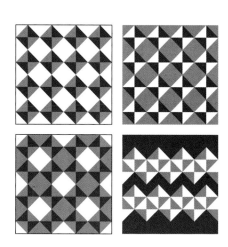

Types of Value Contrast

Usually it is important to have strong value contrast in a quilt design, but there are also beautiful quilts that use low contrast. Whether you are making a quilt with high or low contrast or anywhere in between, what matters is to have *enough* contrast to achieve your intentions for the composition.

High Contrast

High contrast color combinations use drastic steps in value. The quilt design will be most clearly defined when using fabrics with a high degree of contrast. The highest level of contrast is achieved by placing black next to white.

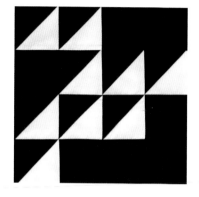

Mid-range Contrast

Most of the time quilters work with contrast somewhere in the middle range. This could be because the majority of commercially produced quilting-weight cotton fabrics are mid-range in value. Having a background (or creating negative space) that contrasts sufficiently with all the other colors in the piecing is often a key element in the design of a successful quilt.

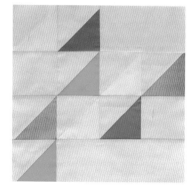

Low Contrast

Low contrast is the pairing of colors with only subtle shifts in value. It can almost make the colors shimmer. Low volume quilts are a variation on this, using fabrics that are pale neutrals with only small hints of other colors. Because the contrast level is low, auditioning fabrics is even more important.

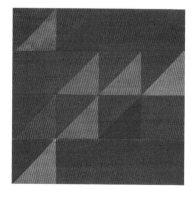

The same block using different levels of contrast (high contrast, left; mid-range contrast, middle; low contrast, right).

Gradation

Gradation is the subtle shift from one hue, saturation level, and/or value to another. Using gradated values gives a sense of depth and creates movement within a quilt. It will make for a smooth and flowing quilt design. It can cause parts of the quilt to pop out as if they were three-dimensional. Gradation requires careful planning and just the right fabrics.

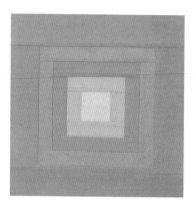

Effective use of gradation.

QUILTER TO QUILTER

The contrast in a quilt can often be amplified by incorporating solid or small-scale tone-on-tone fabrics. For more about piecing with prints, see the Working with Prints workshop on page 40.

Changes in value are easy to see when the hue is removed. It seems that this quilt's design reads well because there are many bold colors. The reality is that the design has clarity because the colors have value contrast. You can see the contrast in value more clearly in the black and white photo. 3/4 Log Cabin by Ara Jane Olufson.

Visualizing Value

Like many quilters, I struggle to see the value in fabrics. The best trick I know to see value is to take a black and white photo. This is a great technique anyone can do. Take a look at the photographs below. I took these photos on my point and shoot camera. I went outside on a bright, sunny day and placed my fabrics on a piece of white poster board, playing around until I thought I had each row in value order. Then I uploaded the photo to my computer and converted it to black and white to check if I was close. I repeated that until I ended up with this arrangement. When you are selecting fabrics, place them together, take a photo in b+w (or in color and then use your favorite photo-editing software to convert it to grayscale), and see if you have enough values with well-defined steps for the quilt you are creating. Photograph all your potential fabrics in consistent light so you don't skew the results. The best way to do this is to group all of them together in the same photo with an even light source.

If taking a photo is not possible, stepping back and squinting also helps. Place your potential fabrics on a design wall or some other place that allows you to see them clearly while you look at them from a distance.

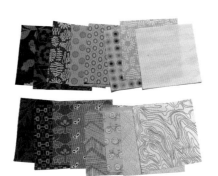
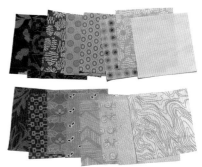

WORKING WITH SATURATION

Being intentional with saturation levels will help your quilt be cohesive. In general, combining many different hues will work more harmoniously if the saturation levels are limited to a small range.

When you are making a quilt with a very limited set of hues varying the saturation levels can keep the quilt from being boring and open up design options.

Highly saturated colors are intense. If you want to reduce their effect, break them up with an ample amount of white, black, gray, or neutral so they are not too overwhelming.

The many tints and tones of blue-green in this quilt add dimension and interest to a restrained palette. Seaglass Herringbone by Claire Jain.

This quilt is a great example of using a variety of colors but maintaining a sense that the colors belong together. The color range has some lighter tones and some darker tones for value contrast. The background colors is are two values of blues that are more desaturated than the blues used in the rest of the quilt. Contact C by Jen Carlton Bailey.

QUILTER TO QUILTER

Audition fabrics that are a few steps darker or lighter than you think you might need; it just might make a good quilt into a great quilt by getting the composition to pop.

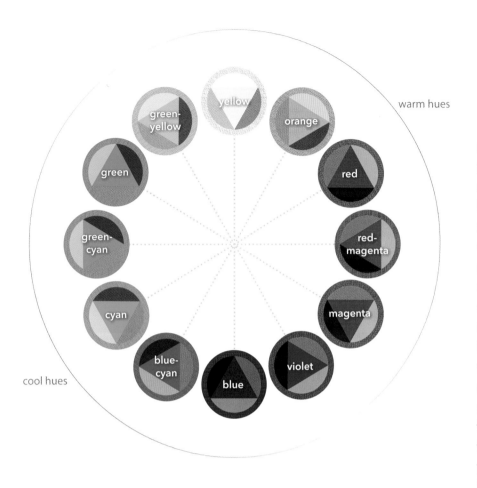

warm hues

cool hues

COLOR WHEEL

One place to turn to when combining hues is the color wheel. The color wheel is basically our visual spectrum wrapped into a circular shape. It can be helpful because it organizes the hues using a logical system that allows us to simplify the relationships the hues have to each other. As I develop successful multiple color schemes, I'll use the color wheel for exploring some classic color relationships.

However, don't feel like you need to justify colors you like together by using the color wheel. There are many cultural and psychological reasons we prefer some color

combinations and not others, many of them unique to the individual. It is also liberating to work intuitively. There are no "one size fits all" solutions to combining hues.

Selecting all the hues of the spectrum, even organizing them in spectral order, can be a fun way to use color in a quilt.

Putting the Color Wheel in Perspective

One of the reasons my students struggle with color selection when

choosing fabrics is not because they are picking hues that are disharmonious on the color wheel, but because something is not right with the saturation levels or value. That's not to say selecting colors based on the color wheel is not useful—it can be—but there is much more to creating a pleasing color palette than simply referencing a color wheel. If you struggle with this, check out the Improvisational Patchwork workshop on page 52, which teaches you to take the decision making out of fabric selection by encouraging you to find unexpected color combinations within your own stash.

The CMY Wheel

I work with the color wheel that uses cyan, magenta, and yellow (CMY) as its primary colors instead of the familiar one that uses blue, red, and yellow. This is because it does a better job at representing the gamut of colors our eyes can see. The blue, red, and yellow wheel is skewed to the warm colors (note that blue, red, and yellow are not evenly spaced on the CMY color wheel). There are more color models, but, to me, this one does the best at combining scientific knowledge with the simplicity of a three-primary-color wheel.

BUILDING A PALETTE

Now that you understand values and saturation, let me walk you through combining hues into a palette of colors for a quilt. Creating a color palette from scratch can be a bit intimidating. The goal when auditioning fabrics for your quilt is to create a palette that has both harmony and interest. Your color choices should be interesting but not chaotic. Where that line is located is different for every quilter and the design goals of each particular quilt.

As you combine hues, you will often choose a palette of tints, shades, and tones, not the pure hues. Keep in mind the values needed to execute the design you have in mind and how the saturation levels are working together for the look you are trying to achieve.

Sometimes palette inspiration comes from another quilt or a favorite fabric print (don't forget to check out the selvedge dots—it's like a premade palette).

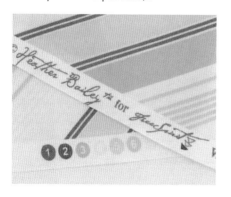

Working with One Hue (Or No Hue!)

Achromatic block.

Monochromatic block.

Achromatic or Grayscale

An achromatic or grayscale color scheme uses a palette of only black, white, and various grays. It can be dramatic or subtle, depending on how many values you choose. It is easy to apply this scheme to a quilt design since you can clearly see changes in value when there is no hue.

Monochromatic

A monochromatic scheme means using one hue and all its varieties to create a quilt design. It is made using tints, shades, and tones of the same hue, along with black, white, and/or gray. Including a variety of values and levels of saturation will keep the design interesting. It is easy to have success with this type of palette since value is still fairly easy to see.

Working with Multiple Hues

Analogous: These colors create a high degree of unity.

Using complementary colors (left) is bolder and creates more energy than using colors that are closer on the color wheel. Note that the colors on the (right) are both cool, which also creates a more subdued effect.

Analogous Schemes

Analogous hues are located next to each other in the color spectrum. Creating your palette by selecting a variety of colors next to each other on the color wheel can give more interest than using just one color, but the palette will still have a high degree of unity.

More unity comes from choosing:
- a smaller part of the spectrum
- more subtle transitions from one color to the next

More interest comes from choosing:
- a bigger part of the spectrum
- larger steps from one color to the next
- a part of the spectrum that transitions from warm to cool (or vice versa)

Two-Hue Schemes

When using two hues, looking at the color wheel becomes more interesting. The farther apart the two colors are on the color wheel, the more energy that color combination will create. The closer the two colors are, the calmer your quilt will be.

Black, White, Gray and Neutrals

Since black, white, and gray are not hues, they can be used with any of these schemes and not count as one of the "colors." I extend that to neutrals, too, although keep in mind that it increases harmony to choose cool neutrals with a dominantly cool scheme and warm neutrals with a dominantly warm scheme.

Temperature

Color has a psychological temperature. Blues, aquas, and greens are considered cool. Yellows, oranges, and reds are considered warm. Unless you create a color scheme that stays on the cool or warm side of the spectrum, you will create interest from the push and pull of color temperatures. Cool colors appear to recede and shrink. Warm colors appear to advance and expand.

QUILTER TO QUILTER

Make a sample block before you cut all your fabric. It's amazing how they look great on a bolt but change when they are sewn together.

Complementary Hues

Colors directly across from each other on the color wheel are called complementary. Using complementary colors is very energetic and intense. You may have to tone down complementary colors by:

- reducing saturation by using tints, shades, and/or tones of the hues.
- breaking the hues up with white, black, gray, or neutrals.

Multiple-Hue Schemes

With more colors added, you can open up design options, but it can also create disharmonious design. Evaluate your saturation if your palette is not working but you want to use many hues. Again, the farther apart your hues are on the color wheel, the more energy the combination will create, especially when highly saturated versions of the colors are used.

Although you can always just pick colors that appeal to you, you may have success working with classical color relationships or exploring the geometry of the color wheel to create your palette.

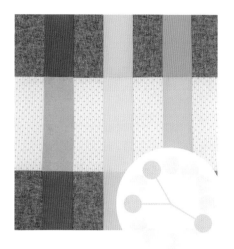

Split complementary: One color plus the two colors on either side of its complement.

Double complementary: Two complementary color pairs.

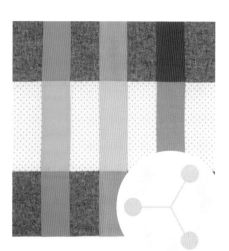

Triad: Three hues equidistant on the color wheel.

Tetrad: Four colors equidistant on the color wheel. Note that this is also made of two complementary pairs.

APPLYING YOUR PALETTE

The amount of negative space and the proportions in which colors are used can completely change their effect. Consider where your colors are being placed in the quilt design when you select fabrics. The proportions should be approached with a sense of purpose for the quilt you are creating.

Playing with the Proportion

Below are four examples of applying the same colors to the same design, with each having a different look. I have selected citron, turquoise, coral, and sea-foam green, with cream as my neutral background.

Can you see how the application of color in **block 1** creates overall vertical stripes that are more noticeable than the individual blocks? The colors create a secondary design. Use even distribution of colors to achieve equal dominance between the colors in the palette.

In **block 2**, the turquoise is dominant but there is still the added color dimension of the rest of my color palette. I have used varying proportions for each color to create interest.

In **block 3** the colors are less intense than in the other examples because of the addition of sashing. The use of negative space will change the intensity of a color palette. Using neutrals, white, gray, or black will give the eye a place to rest.

By taking my palette and paring it down to just two colors **(block 4)**, I have created a bold focal point. Using this technique can create a visually striking secondary design in a quilt. Small amounts of contrast color can liven up a quilt design, while using it evenly might be either too overwhelming or too boring. The contrast color will grab your attention, so be purposeful with its application.

Get Courageous with Color

When choosing colors, there are no formulas that must be followed. These foundational concepts are a guide to using color with more understanding, but are flexible. They create possibilities for you to express your own artistic vision. Practice and a mind open to experimentation are the best ways to gain skill and confidence. Get creative and have fun with color!

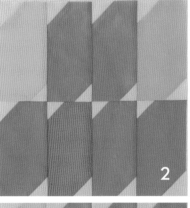

Carolyn Friedlander's Aerial quilt (left) uses a multitude of colors successfully. Tints and tones from all over the color wheel could easily get overwhelming. The main reason they work so well in this quilt is because Carolyn skillfully grouped the colors in block units instead of mixing them in every block. This reigns in the chaos of using so many colors and creates structure and movement. The repetition of the block form unifies the quilt, as does the mix of solid or nearly solid fabrics.

TROUBLESHOOTING GUIDE

Here is a quick reference list of ideas to try if something isn't working with the colors you've selected. Sometimes just changing one thing can make all the difference.

NOT HARMONIOUS?

• Remove a color.

• Adjust the proportions in your palette to have one color dominant and the others playing a supporting role.

• Choose colors with a similar saturation level (for example, very saturated or desaturated) and type of saturation (tints, shades or tones).

• Consult a color wheel and consider shifting your hues.

• Break up colors by adding in more white, black, gray, or neutrals.

• Group each hue together instead of mixing the hues together. For example, create one block that is red and another that is yellow instead of two blocks that are both red and yellow.

MUDDLED DESIGN?

Increase value contrast by selecting darker fabrics for the darks and/or lighter fabrics for the lights, plus larger steps in value for all middle-range values.

• Add in more solid, small-scale, and/or tone-on-tone fabrics.

TOO BORING?

• Add in pops of an additional color, especially from the opposite side of the color wheel.

• Give the design more depth by increasing contrast (make lights lighter, darks darker). Use varying saturations. Add slight shifts within a basic hue (for example: for green, include fabrics that go a few steps more blue and a few steps more yellow).

• Add in some larger scale prints or fabrics with more contrast in the print.

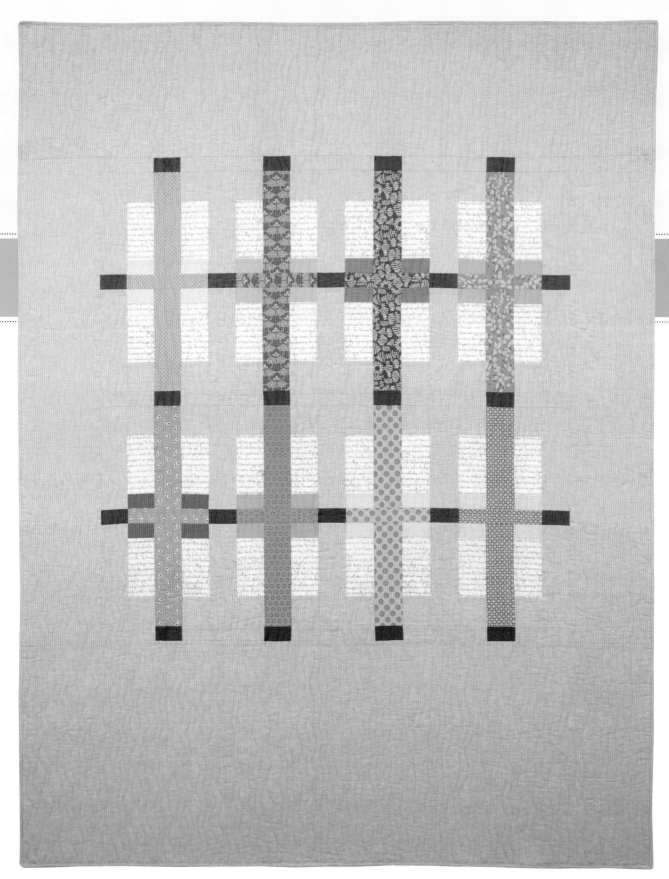

Quilted by Susan Santistevan

COLOR PLAY

Experiment with color with this simple and versatile quilt pattern. It looks great with both a very limited color palette or with tons of colors. The value placement can be successfully changed, too.

FINISHED QUILT SIZE: 57½" × 71¼"
FINISHED BLOCK SIZE: 7½" × 18¾"

MATERIALS

4 yards of background fabric

⅛ yard each of 8 print fabrics

⅛ yard (or two 5" charm squares) each of 8 solid accent fabrics

½ yard of white text fabric

⅛ yard of olive cornerstone fabric

CUTTING THE FABRIC

1. From the background fabric, use the cutting diagram (below) to cut the following:

☐ One 58" strip. From this strip, cut one 19 ¼" × 58" border and one 11¾" × 58" border. From the remainder, cut thirty-two 3" squares.

☐ One 41¾" strip. From this strip, cut two 8" × 41¾" borders. From the remainder, cut twenty 3" × 9¼" rectangles, nine 1¾" × 8" rectangles, and six 1¾" × 5½" rectangles.

2. From each of the eight print fabrics, cut two 3" × 9 ¼" rectangles and one 1¾" × 8" rectangle.

3. From each of the eight solid accent fabrics, cut four 1¾" × 3" rectangles.

4. From the white text fabric, cut five 3" strips. Cut these into thirty-two 3" × 5½" rectangles.

5. From the olive cornerstone fabric, cut one 3" strip. Cut this into twenty-two 1¾" × 3" rectangles.

6. From the binding fabric, cut seven 2½" strips.

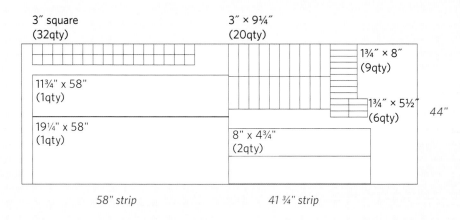

Background fabric cutting diagram

MAKING THE BLOCKS

To make one block, gather a set of two 3" × 9¼" rectangles and one 1¾" × 8" rectangle of print fabric, four coordinating 1¾" × 3" solid accent rectangles, four 3" × 5½" text rectangles and, four 3" squares of background fabric.

1. Referring to the corner unit diagram **(Fig. 2)**, sew one 1¾" × 3" rectangle of solid accent fabric to a 3" × 5½" rectangle of text fabric. Next sew a 3" square of background fabric to the other end

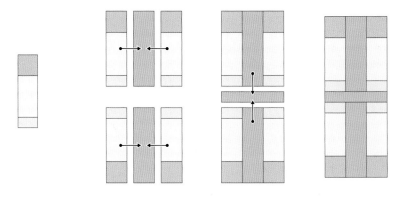

Figure 2   Figure 3

of the text fabric to make a block corner unit. Repeat to assemble all four corner units.

2. Referring to the block assembly diagram **(Fig. 3)**, sew two corner units to one 3" × 9¼" rectangle of print fabric to form top row of block. Repeat for second set of corner units to form bottom row of block. Sew the top and bottom row to the remaining 1¾" × 8" rectangle of print fabric, oriented so that edges with the solid accents are sewn to the center rectangle of colorful print fabric. The block should measure 8" × 19¼".

3. Repeat Steps 1 and 2 with the remaining sets to make eight blocks.

ASSEMBLING THE CENTER

1. Sew horizontal sashing rows together. The rows are assembled in the order indicated **(Fig. 4)**. Repeat to make three horizontal sashing strips. Set aside.

2. Sew vertical sashing units together. Sew one 3" × 9¼" rectangle of background fabric to each side of one cornerstone. Repeat to make ten vertical sashing units.

3. Sew vertical sashing units to blocks to form two rows.

4. Sew horizontal sashing rows to block rows to complete quilt top center.

FINISHING THE QUILT

1. Referring to the quilt top assembly diagram **(Fig. 5)**, sew one 8" × 41¾" border to each side of the quilt center.

2. Sew the 11¾" × 58" border to the top and the 19¼" × 58" border to the bottom to complete the top.

3. Piece the backing to 66" × 79". Layer backing, batting, and quilt top; baste and quilt as desired.

4. Piece the binding strips together with diagonal seams. Fold the binding strip in half, wrong sides together, and press. Bind the quilt using a ¼" seam allowance.

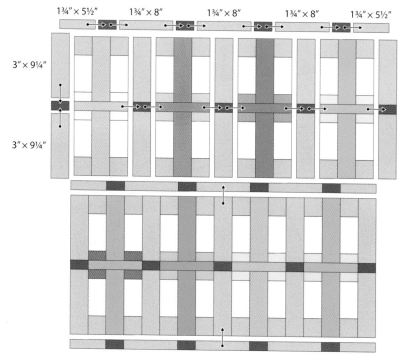

Figure 4

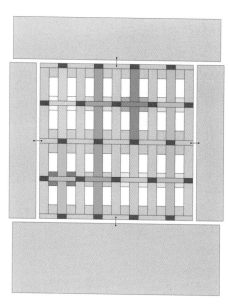

Figure 5

WORKING WITH SOLIDS

A DESIGN WORKSHOP

Goal of the class: Use this workshop to experiment with the possibilities that solid fabrics have to offer modern quilters. If you are new to improv piecing, the accompanying pattern to my workshop is a simple one to begin with. If you are used to piecing with the beautiful printed fabrics available today, this workshop is an opportunity to push your boundaries and use solids to bring contrast, line, texture, and negative space into your compositions.

TEACHER:
Alissa Haight Carlton

WHAT SOLIDS HAVE TO OFFER

Solid fabrics really add so much to a quilt. Those prints that you're in love with? Solids will make them look even better! The more I've worked with solids, the more I've learned what they can contribute to a design. If you don't consider them as an effective option in your piecing, you're not using one of the biggest design tools available to you.

SOLIDS IN THE DESIGN PROCESS

Using solids add polish and calm to your design. If you put a large number of prints next to one another, your eye will naturally crave a place to rest. Solids can provide that resting place in your design. I can't appreciate a print as much if it is right next to another one with no room to breathe. In my classes, I encourage my students to add solid fabrics to their work when they might have reached for a print instead, and take the time to notice how the print and solid fabric complement one another.

As you grow your quilting voice, I encourage you to explore using solids and constantly experiment with the balance of solid and printed fabrics within your own designs. Even if you are a firm lover of prints, challenge yourself!

If you are new to working with solids, have fun experimenting with different types, as I describe later. Many quilters are drawn to printed fabrics first; this workshop is about encouraging students to creatively push themselves by doing something outside their comfort zones and really noticing what happens to piecing when they select a solid instead of a print. It's about adding another option to your toolbox.

QUILTER TO QUILTER

Why not make the pattern I designed for this workshop without including a single print? Or just feature one big fun pop of print, like I did with the orange scrap.

TYPES OF SOLIDS

It may seem that solids lack variety. A solid is a solid, right? But that's not the case in fabrics. There are a number of different types of solid fabrics that add richness and depth to your quilt in different ways. Let's work our way through the existing options so that you learn how many choices there really are. Understanding these differences will allow you to see the fabric options available to you that go beyond just color. Because there are many more fabric types than I can list here, I'll focus specifically on commercially available quilting cottons.

True solid quilting cotton.

True Solids

What most of my students think of when I say "solid" is the most common type: the true solid.

Woven fabrics have threads running through them in two directions, vertically and horizontally. These are called the warp and weft threads. The warp is made up of the long vertical threads that the horizontal weft threads are woven back and forth through. A true solid is a fabric in which the warp

Crossweaves as solids.

and weft thread color, thickness, and texture are identical. There is a very graphic and open feeling to true solids. Depending on the fiber type and specific weave, true solid fabrics can be shiny, but most quilting cottons are matte. The modern quilter uses matte true solids extensively.

Crossweaves

Unlike true solids, a crossweave has different colors of thread in its warp and weft. Sometimes the thread colors are very different from each other, and sometimes they are just a few shades or hues off from the same color. This can give the fabric an iridescent look when the cloth moves in the light.

No matter what the mix is, the addition of a different thread woven into the fabric produces a beautiful depth and dimension to the fabric.

Textured Solids

Loose linen weaves, nubs and bumps, and all kinds of different fibers are sometimes included in the thread that fabric is woven with. In a textured solid fabric, while the colors of the warp and weft are the same, the threads (or fibers) of the fabric have little bumps and lumps of texture. When woven together, this gives

Textured solids with mixed fibers.

the fabric an added dimension that provides tactile appeal. Some fabric manufacturers also print subtle textured patterns directly onto the fabric to mimic this woven look.

CHOOSING SOLIDS FOR A QUILT

Choosing the fabric you're going to use in a quilt is one of the most fulfilling parts of the quilting process. When making these decisions, there are a number of factors I advise my students to consider.

Color

Most important is, of course, color. Color tastes are hugely subjective, and making color choices that work well for the specific design you are piecing is a major part of the creative process of quilting. Developing strong color preferences is one element of finding your own artistic voice. I encourage students to spend time with

their fabric and relish growing their stash. Your stash is likely the greatest indicator of the hues and tones you are naturally drawn to.

When it comes to buying solids, you have every color of the rainbow available. There's nothing more inspiring to me than having access to many options to audition as I pull colors for a new design.

In my workshops, I often remind students that the eye needs a place to rest, not only from prints, but also from bold color. Consider including neutrals in an otherwise bold, bright, and colorful quilt to really give those colors a setting they can shine in.

QUILTER TO QUILTER

Solids are often less expensive than printed fabric, so don't hesitate to add a nice selection to your stash. Some of my favorites are Robert Kaufman Kona Cottons, Kaffe Fassett's Shot Cottons, Moda's Crossweaves, In the Beginning's Modern Solids (my own collection), and Andover's Textured Solids.

Value

Another important part of fabric selection is value. Value is also discussed in detail in The Principles of Color workshop on page 6. The trick I turn to as I mix and match my stacks of fabric is to squint when looking at the stacks.

By doing this, any big value differences pop right out when you are auditioning a collection of fabrics together.

COMPOSITION

Using solids makes you focus on the composition of the piecing design. This is why improvisational piecing with solids works so wonderfully. Rather than creating the pattern or interest in your piecing by relying on prints, you allow the contrast to be created by a variety of tones, hues, and values. There are a number of compositional factors to consider when designing a quilt using solids:

Symmetry or Asymmetry?

Every quilter is different; my students are drawn to a variety of compositions. Personally, I am drawn to asymmetry in my design, but that's not something all modern quilters feel. I like the off-kilter and unpredictable and tend to include asymmetry in my designs in more than one way. I'll usually set the overall composition so that the focal point is not centered, then take it a step further by introducing asymmetrical fabric placement.

Many modern quilters focus on symmetry in their designs, where the focal point is centered and

Bias 2 features asymmetry.

Symmetric quilt by Heather Jones.

often repeated in a grid, especially if the design is block based. No matter what style you prefer, relying on solids to create interest and movement in your composition will result in balanced and well-presented designs.

Concave or Convex?

Another compositional choice that I discuss with my students is what shapes they are drawn to. Do they like concave bends more than convex? Do they like when shapes poke out of or into the

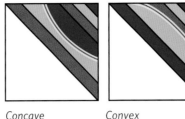

Concave   *Convex*

overall design? I personally prefer concave to convex, but there's not really a rhyme or reason to it that I can explain. It's just what I like! It's only in the doing (the designing, making, piecing and sewing together bits of fabric for hours and hours on end) that you'll develop

your own voice and determine what shapes call your name.

Straight or Not So Perfectly Straight Lines?

Do you like perfectly straight and uniform lines, or do you prefer the more organic look and feel that improv piecing can provide? This use of line in a composition is something to pay attention to and use to your advantage to create the look, mood, and reaction you want your design to convey.

IMPROVISATIONAL PIECING

Improvisational piecing means just what it sounds like: cutting and sewing in a loose and fun way. This improv style of quilting is explored further in the Improvisational Patchwork workshop on page 52. It keeps the design process going through the labor of the piecing. If you've never tried it, starting can be daunting so it's good to dive in by working on a more structured project includes just one improv aspect. I tell my students that the best way to get started is to simply do it. Just start sewing, and keep sewing. The more you improv-piece, the more you'll find your own rhythm and voice.

Improvisationally pieced block.

NEGATIVE SPACE

In modern quilting, many of the quilt designs include expansive negative space. Negative space is the portion of the quilt design that is secondary to the primary design and is usually free of pattern. When creating negative space, your composition will often be more successful if you use a solid fabric. If you use a print for this part of the quilt design, it's likely to detract from the overall composition and can change the intent of the background, making it more prominent to the eye.

QUILTER — TO QUILTER

I find that one (or three, but usually not two) little pops of a contrasting fabric can be the extra detail that adds so much to a composition. The quilt project I've created for this workshop is a great example of this.

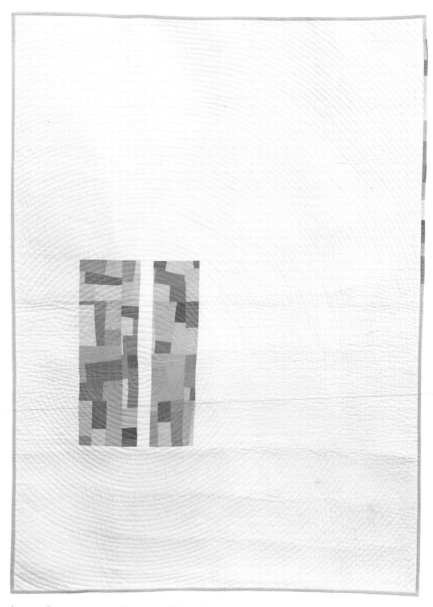

Improv Bars uses negative space effectively.

WHAT ARE THE FIBERS?

All of the fabrics I've mentioned in this workshop are woven using either 100% cotton or a cotton/linen blend of fibers. Fabrics produced using these two types of fiber are what I have utilized pretty much exclusively in my own quilting. Of course, garment sewers work with many other types of fabrics with a variety of fiber content, but for the most part, modern quilters stick to using fabrics with 100% cotton fiber or cotton/linen blends.

FEATURING PRINTS

Another tool to add to your design toolbox is to make prints really sing by surrounding them with solids. Take this quilt of mine as an example.

The quilt pictured right is one in a series of quilts made with the "greater than" symbol idea. My intent was to feature one fabric line, Jay McCarroll's Center City. I knew that these prints would become much more prominent by surrounding them with solids. Some improv piecing, mixed with a very large open space of background fabric (negative space), really lets the prints shine.

I encourage you to play with all of these compositional concepts by selecting a solid fabric instead of a print in your next design. Solids have the ability to add texture; to guide the eye across a design; to reflect line, shape, and contrast without the distraction of a print; or even complement the prints you love. You may not turn to working with solids almost exclusively, but I hope this workshop will help you understand and embrace all of the possibilities solids can bring to your work as you develop your own quilting voice.

Negative space highlights feature prints well.

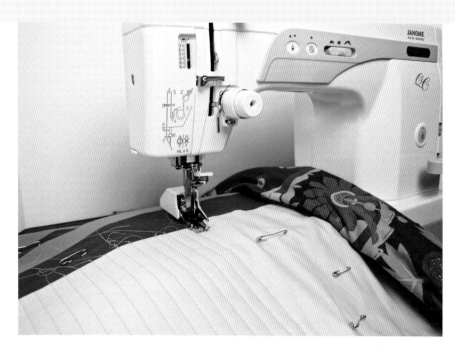

Janome's High Speed Straight Stitch 1600P-QC is perfect for straight line quilting.

STRAIGHT-LINE QUILTING

I straight-line quilt almost all of my quilts and have learned a lot from my experience. Here are some tips:

1. Spend plenty of time and energy on basting. The more thoroughly you baste, the less you'll deal with the issues caused by shifting fabric.

2. Use a walking foot or your machine's equivalent. This helps the layers of the "quilt sandwich" feed smoothly through your machine.

3. If your machine has an adjustable presser foot, adjust it so that it isn't pushing as firmly as you would have it set for piecing. You want the fabric to feed through without being pushed around.

4. Think through the order in which you're going to work your way through the quilt. You want to work from the center out as much as possible so that should the fabric shift, it can be smoothed.

5. If you need to stop and start in the middle of the quilt, make sure you sew a locking stitch or two so that everything stays in place over time. When you stop and when you start, you'll want to leave long thread tails. Eventually you will either trim them, or of this is a quilt that you want to go the extra mile for, bury them.

6. Putting in a new bobbin before you get started is worth taking the time to do.

7. You need a way to make sure that your first line is straight. I often find that I can use piecing as my guide, but if you don't have that option, draw the first line with chalk or a fabric pen or use painter's tape as a guide to follow.

8. One option for denser spacing between your quilting lines is to use the edge of your machine's foot as the guide for each consecutive line you sew.

9. If you don't want to quilt as densely as the width of your machine's foot, use a quilting bar to create uniform straight lines any width you prefer.

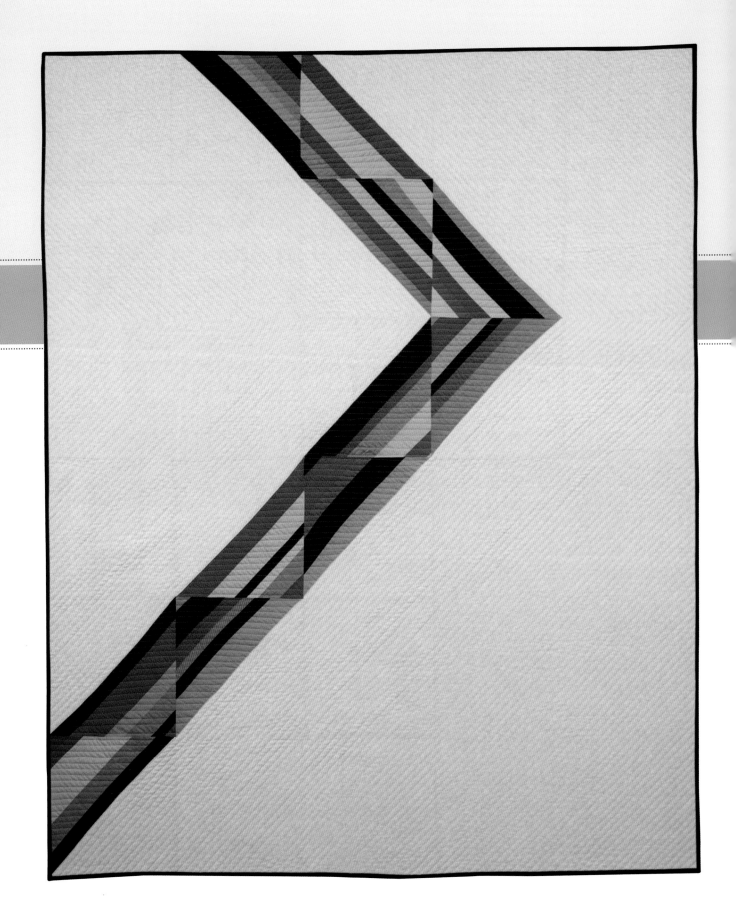

GREATER THAN

This pattern is created by making a few blocks and arranging them within negative space. Since each block is improvisationally pieced, each one is different. As a result, even though the primary design of the quilt is the same, no two quilt tops will be identical. Just a few contrasting solid fabrics, pieced together, create the graphic and modern look of this quilt.

FINISHED QUILT SIZE: 60" × 72"

MATERIALS

3⅔ yards of background fabric

A total of 2 yards combined of at least four different fabrics in ¼-yard cuts or scraps of various widths, some at least 22" long

4 yards of backing fabric

½ yard of binding fabric

68" × 80" batting

12½" square acrylic ruler

CUTTING THE FABRIC

1. From the background fabric, cut the following:

☐ Three 15" strips. Cut these into six 15" squares (A1–A6), then cut each square once diagonally from corner to corner to make twelve triangles for the eleven block backgrounds (toss the extra triangle in your scrap bin). These triangles have long bias edges, so take care to not stretch the edges.

☐ Cut three 12½" strips. Cut two of these into four 12½" squares (Units A7–A10). Trim the third strip to 12½" × 36½" (Unit A11).

☐ Cut one 24½" strip. From this, cut one 12½" × 24½" rectangle (Unit A12). Trim the rest of that strip to 24½" × 24½" (Unit A13). You are left with a 25" wide piece of fabric. Trim it to a 24½" × 36½" rectangle (Unit A14).

2. Cut ¼ yard cuts or scraps of fabrics into strips, varying the widths from 1½" to 3" and the lengths between 5" for the shortest strips and 22" for the longest. Longer strips can be trimmed after the block is pieced.

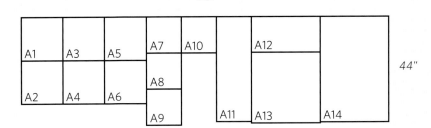

Background fabric cutting diagram.

FABRIC SUGGESTIONS

When picking fabric, be certain that there is a lot of contrast between the piecing fabrics and the background fabric. This pattern will work well in any number of color choices. I decided to go with lots of grays, navy, and one fun pop of a vivid orange, but almost any combo with bright fun colors will work.

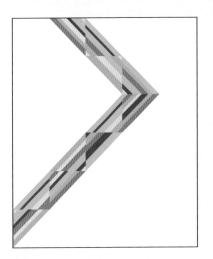

Why not go scrappy and use colors from your scrap bin and stash?

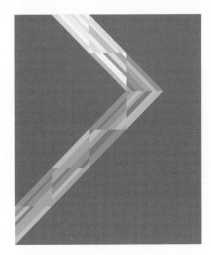

Or how about all teals and aquas with some warm yellows?

MAKING THE BLOCKS

1. Sew one long strip along the long bias edge of one background triangle (cut diagonally from units A1- A6). Again, be careful not to stretch the bias edge. Press.

2. Continue adding strips, pressing seams open as you go, until the block is larger than 12½" square. In order to do this in a truly improvisational manner, just grab a strip that's a different color and sew it on. Don't think too much. If you work this way for a number of blocks, you'll see that the impact of all the blocks together is wonderful and each small individual decision matters less. Use the

triangle portion of the block to see how long the next contrasting strip should be. Err on the side of sewing on a strip that is too long, rather than one that is too short. Make sure to mix colors, widths of strips, and textures of fabrics.

3. Square up the block. Use a 12 ½" square ruler: align the seam between the background triangle and pieced triangle along the 45-degree line, square up the block.

4. Repeat Steps 1 through 3 to make a total of eleven 12½" × 12½" blocks.

QUILTER TO QUILTER

Try to push yourself outside of your comfort zone as you cut. If you've never done any improvisational cutting, try using your ruler, but not the lines on your mat. If you're more comfortable working in this style, do away with the ruler altogether! Just cut your fabrics while eyeballing a straight line. This will lead to intentionally askew cuts and give the finished improvisational piecing a look that is organic and beautiful.

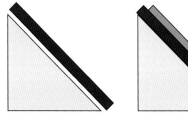

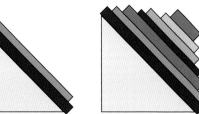

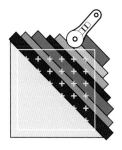

Steps for individual block assembly.ww

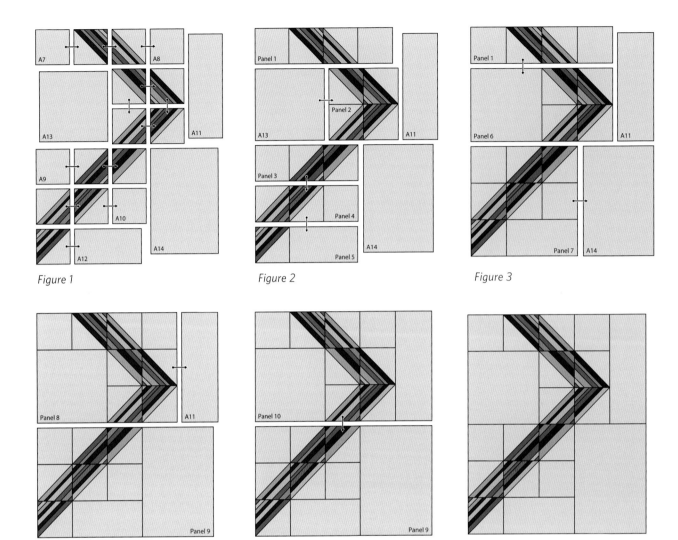

Figure 1

Figure 2

Figure 3

Figure 4

Figure 5

Figure 6

ASSEMBLING THE QUILT TOP

1. Lay out the pieced blocks and background Units A1-A8.

2. Referencing **Figure 1**, begin assembling the pieced block units in the following order pressing all seams open:

- Sew A7, two pieced blocks, and A8 into a row (Panel 1).
- Sew four pieced blocks into Panel 2.

- Sew A9 and two pieced blocks into a row (Panel 3).
- Sew two pieced blocks and A10 into a row (Panel 4).
- Sew one pieced block and A12 into a row (Panel 5).

3. Referencing **Figure 2**, sew Panel 2 and A13 together to create Panel 6. Sew Panels 3, 4, and 5 together to create Panel 7 pressing all seams open.

4. Referencing **Figure 3 and 4**, create Panels 8 and 9 pressing all seams open.

5. Referencing **Figure 5**, create Panel 10, pressing all seams open, to complete the top half of the quilt.

6. Sew Panel 10 to Panel 9, pressing all seams open, to complete the quilt top **(Fig. 6)**.

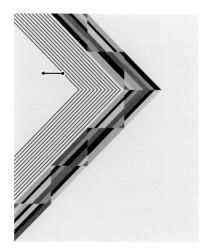

Figure 7

Figure 8

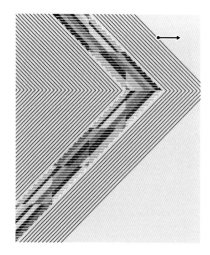

Figure 9

FINISHING THE QUILT

1. Piece the backing fabric to 68" × 80". Layer the backing, batting, and quilt top; baste the layers together.

2. If you'd like to replicate my quilting, refer to **Figure 7**. First stitch along the inner edge of the piecing. Next, use the edge of the walking foot as a guide to echo-quilt that first line. Work towards the left, filling in the pieced area **(Fig. 8)**.

Fill in the improve piecing with back and forth parallel lines using the edge of your foot as a guide.

Finally, use the same technique to fill in the right side of the quilt top, one line at a time **(Fig. 9)**. After the top is completely quilted, square up the backing and batting.

3. Choosing the binding fabric is the final creative decision for the quilt.

How do you want the design to be framed? Floating without seeing the binding? A strong contrasting frame? Asking these questions will help you decide which fabric to chose. If my students really struggle with this, I advise them to go with the darkest fabric in their quilt top as it will act as a frame. I prefer to use solids throughout my quilts, all the way down to the binding.

For a quilt top with a lot of solids, you could consider using a small-scale print. A binding that has a small stripe or little polka dot is a great juxtaposition to the solids in a quilt.

4. To bind, cut seven 2½" strips and join with diagonal seams and bind using your preferred method.

QUILTER TO QUILTER

In a design with this much negative space, quilting is key to the final look. Consider adding to the already graphic nature of the solids in the top with a repeating, dense straight-line quilting motif that echoes the pieced design. This type of quilting takes a lot of time, but the texture gained in the finished result is worth it. See page 33 for more tips on straight-line quilting.

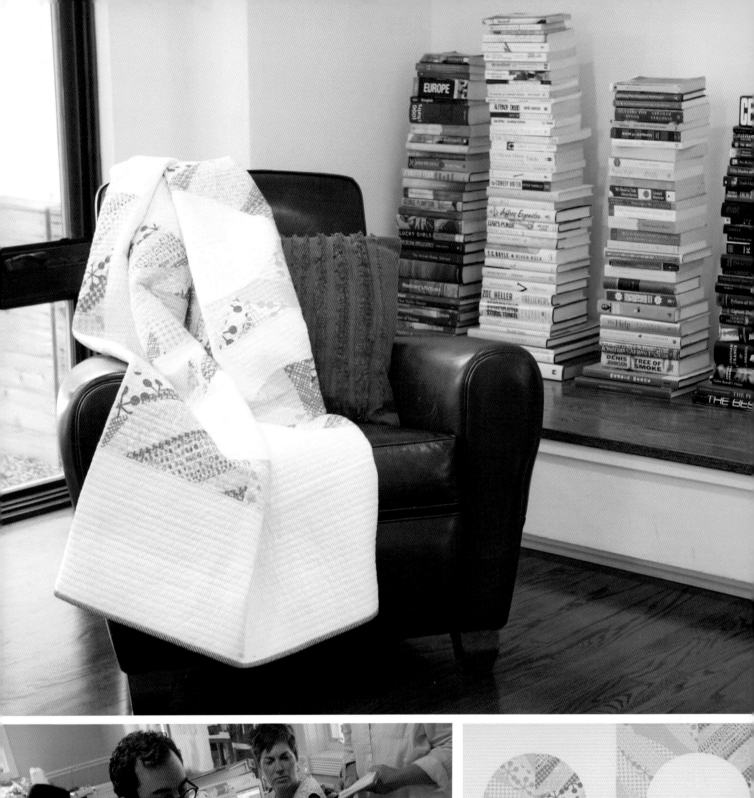

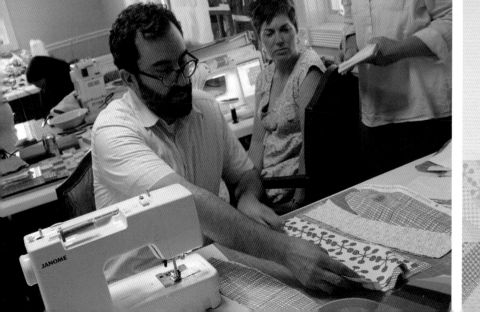

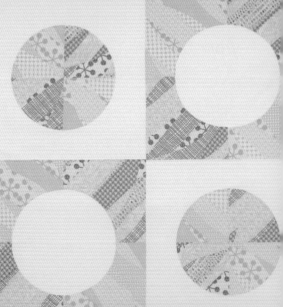

WORKING WITH PRINTS

A DESIGN WORKSHOP

Goal of the class: Use this workshop to experiment with the possibilities that printed fabrics have to offer modern quilters. If you usually work with solids, try integrating prints to add visual interest to your designs. By understanding how the scale of print, the value, and the size of the pieced units impact the composition, you can create a design in which prints and solids work together to direct the eye.

TEACHER:
Dan
Rouse

Prints in Modern Quilts

I love to use prints in my quilts for several reasons. At the simplest level, a print can capture a memory or association in a way that a solid can't. I associate prints not only with the creative process of making a given quilt, but also with my participation in the greater quilting community: the shop where I bought the print, the other quilts and textiles I've seen using the print in similar and different ways, the moment the fabric seemed stylish and maybe even the moment it didn't seem so stylish. These associations work as personal markers of my creative experience, but also as signposts for others who view the quilts.

WHAT PRINTS HAVE TO OFFER

From a design standpoint, prints offer visual depth and softness. While a large field of solid color can create sharpness and clarity (as discussed in the Working with Solids workshop on page 24), the color will have the same appearance close up and far away. Of course the closer you get, the more you will see texture and the qualities of the construction and the materials, but a print offers the added richness of drawn elements. Stand close and the individual scrap contains its own story. Take a step back and the print starts a conversation with its neighboring fabrics. Stand back four more steps and the individual prints begin to disappear into larger elements of color and value.

QUILTER TO QUILTER

I sometimes mix a handful of similarly colored prints with several similarly colored solids, allowing the prints to stand out a bit as individuals, even as they blend into a unified color field.

PRINTS AS PART OF THE DESIGN PROCESS

My projects almost always begin with a design idea for the quilt as a whole, and then I find fabrics that serve the overall design. Fabrics shine when they contribute to a strong design. This approach is informed by my professional experience as a landscape designer. When I design a landscape, I start with the fattest possible pencil and sketch landscape areas and human circulation, imagining the way I want people to feel as they pass through the space. The very last thing I think about is specific surface and plant materials. While those things are important and create charm and interest, the spatial relationships are what determine the success or failure of a landscape. Similarly, the design of a quilt comes first, and the fabrics are chosen to serve that design.

NEGATIVE SPACE

In modern quilting, it's usually assumed that negative space is defined by white or neutral solids. It is analogous to the concept of "white space" in print media. I take a more expansive view in my quilt design and encourage my students to do the same. Negative space serves as the background to the subject of a design. That background doesn't have to be blank; it can have texture, color, variation, and interest. The trick is that the interest has to be secondary to the subject of the quilt.

Partly Cloudy by Alexandra Ledgerwood.

Creating Negative Space Using Prints

One strategy for creating negative space using prints is to use many prints of similar color, combined to create larger fields that read as one distinct area when viewed from a distance. This works best when fabrics share a dominant color, though it is not necessary (or even desirable) for the prints to be monochromatic. It also helps if the scale of each print is in the fine to medium range, so that the individual print shapes are recognizable up close and obscured when viewed from several paces.

In the context of an overall quilt design, negative space constructed in this way frames the chosen subject of a composition and provides a place for the eye to rest. Additionally, it contributes a secondary level of color, richness, and texture.

Creating Positive Space Using Prints

It's also possible to create positive space – the subject or design foreground of the quilt – in the same way. When both the foreground and background of a quilt are constructed from prints, there are a host of design strategies to create clarity in the composition.

Build up a stash of colors you love to work with when buying prints.

DEFINE THE SUBJECT USING CONTRAST

To achieve a successful design, it is essential to have contrast whether you are using prints or solids. The stronger and simpler the contrast, the easier it is to read the subject of the design. With more levels or gradation of contrast, the design becomes more delicate and achieves a sense of depth, but can also be more complex and perhaps more convoluted. A high level of contrast clearly defines positive and negative space, ideally giving a sense of foreground and background.

You can achieve contrast in a variety of ways. The most important strategy is to present a strong visual form. Be sure you

can see the outlines of your intended shapes. Then use what you learned in the Principles of Color workshop on page 6 to further distinguish positive and negative space through contrast in value, saturation, and hue. Depending on your design goals, you don't have to use all three strategies.

THE POWER OF VARIATION

Variation in value is a powerful and dependable technique. You will perceive the contrast between light and dark quickly, and viewers will sort the difference between foreground and background without effort.

Building up a good stash of fabric options over time will help ensure variety. Because you may have trouble finding enough closely matching fabrics on the shelves at the same time. It works better to identify the colors you like to work with, and purchase fabrics when you find them in the right range of color and scale.

When colors match too closely, the effect can be visually deadening. Variation can give your eye a reason to move and find excitement in the composition. When building your stash, concentrate on finding those values that you use most often in your work instead of focusing on the print itself. Select prints that play with one or two different tones or hues within that value.

SCALE

The scale of a print can have a tremendous impact on a quilt. Small-scale prints can read as solids, while large-scale prints can read as piecing. I tend to use small-scale prints precisely because I love the way they read at a distance as solids and grow more lively as you approach the quilt. Using a variety of prints, each fabric will have a threshold where the individual design becomes recognizable relative to the other prints—six paces, four paces, two feet, six inches—and I find that evolving detail very exciting and encourage my students to play with that concept in my classes.

FIND YOUR RHYTHM

Rhythm is a key quality in a compelling design. Your composition has the power to control how people see your quilt, the order in which they see elements, and the speed at which their eye passes from one element to the next. By arranging the design elements of your quilt with a sense of rhythm, you direct the viewer's eye across and around the quilt and create a sense of energy and movement in a static object.

Varying the distribution of print scale within your quilt—from solid to small, medium or large-scale —will direct the viewer's eye. Keep the viewer's eye moving around your quilt by distributing your

Sketch out designs before selecting fabrics.

QUILTER TO QUILTER

Next time you are tempted to use a large piece of a large-scale fabric in a design, try using a combination of smaller pieces instead. Notice how this can complement the overall composition instead of focusing the eye on the individual fabric.

standout fabrics in an interesting way across the compostion.

Think about having a background and a foreground in your composition. The background will be whatever you have the most of which actually makes a weaker statement.

INSPIRATION

I never start a quilt design with a specific print or fabric collection in mind. With very few exceptions, I have a clear idea what I want the quilt to look like before I consider a single fabric. You can try this by sketching out the design first and defining the composition. Ask yourself where you want to create foreground and background, how you want the eye to move across the quilt, etc. When you begin here, the fabric combination can truly support the design to achieve the goals of the composition.

SKYLIGHTS

This quilt combines improvisational curved piecing with traditional geometry in the larger composition.

We'll use a stack and cut method to create "made fabric", or strata. The strata is created as a preliminary step, effectively building the raw material fabric for piecing the quilt. You'll build the strata without knowing where each improve curve or intersection will appear in the final composition. Your goal will be to create an even, composition of compatible prints.

FINISHED QUILT SIZE: 66" × 85"
FINISHED BLOCK SIZE: 11" × 11"

MATERIALS

6 yellow print fat quarters

6 orange print fat quarters

4 yards of white solid

5/8 yard of binding fabric

5½ yards of backing fabric

74" × 93" batting

CUTTING THE FABRIC

1. From the white solid, cut the following:

☐ Four 11½" strips. Cut these into twelve 11½" × 11½" squares. Use Template A (see page 191) to remove a quarter circle from one corner of each square for the concave block pieces.

☐ Three 7½" strips. Cut these into twelve 7½" × 7½" squares. Use Template B (see page 191) to trim the squares into quarter circles for the convex block pieces.

☐ One 11½" × 66½" top strip (cut lengthwise). One 30½" × 66½" bottom strip (cut lengthwise).

2. From the binding, cut eight 2½" strips.

BUILDING THE STRATA

1. Stack six yellow fat quarters on a cutting mat with the 18" edge at the bottom. Using a rotary cutter with a sharp blade, make five gently curved cuts from bottom to top to create six stacks of curved strips **(Fig. 1)**.

2. Divide the strips into six sets—one strip from each strip stack and from each fat quarter. A good way to do this is to methodically shuffle your fabric stacks. Leave the first pile as-is. For the second pile, move the top piece of fabric to the bottom of the stack. For the third pile, move the top two pieces of fabric to the bottom of the stack, and so on.

3. To make one curvy yellow block of fabric, sew the five strips from one set together to form a block approximately 18" × 19½" **(Fig. 2)**. Press each seam to the inside of the curve.

4. Repeat Step 3 for the remaining 5 sets.

5. Take the six curvy yellow blocks and stack them on the cutting mat with the corresponding seams in each block more or less aligned.

6. Cut the blocks again as in Step 1, intersecting the new cuts with the completed seams **(Fig. 3)**. Avoid creating tiny fragments of prints that will get lost in seam allowances.

7. Repeat Steps 2 through 4, aiming for a fairly even distribution of prints in each block.

8. Sew blocks again as in Step 3 to make six yellow blocks approxiamately 17" x 18" **(Fig. 4)**.

9. Arrange Templates A and B (see page 191) on point creating a diamond shape for each block. Leaving an extra ¼" margin all around the templates, roughly cut out the convex and concave parts of the block. You will come back in Step 11 and precisely trim the block after a second pressing. First do an initial rough cut, a second press, and a final cut to get precise results.

10. Press the pieces again.

11. Return to the cutting mat and use Templates A and B to carefully trim the rough cuts you made in Step 8.

12. Repeat Steps 1 through 11 with orange fat quarters.

Figure 1

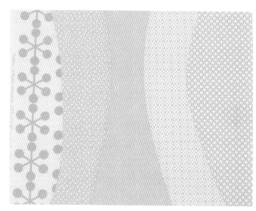
Figure 2

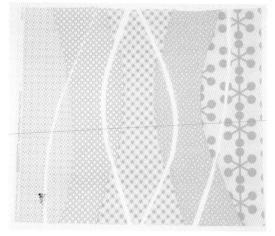
Figure 3

Figure 4

SEWING THE STRATA CURVES

- Don't pin, but sew slowly.

- Begin with right sides together and the edges aligned at the start of the seam. Don't worry about matching edges farther along. Aim for a ¼" seam and sew three or four stitches at a time.

- Hold each fabric in a different hand, 3" or 4" in front of the needle. Use both hands to keep the seam allowance consistent directly in front of the needle. Don't worry about the rest of the seam!

- Don't pull on the fabrics. Bias edges along the curve can distort easily.

- At the end of the seam, check the fabric edges. There is no need to be perfect, but a closer match will be easier to work with later. If the fabric edges are out of alignment, adjust the way you guide the next pair of strips through the machine. A very small amount of tension can make a big difference along an 18" seam.

- Cut a nice easy curve without changing directions during the cut.

- Use a 6" × 24" ruler to hold the fabric stack steady while cutting.

Finished Concave and Convex Blocks.

MAKING THE BLOCKS

1. Fold a white concave piece (Template A) in half diagonally, matching the ends of the curve. Fold in half again, matching the center of the curve with the edges. Press creases in the seam allowance to mark the quarter points along the curve. Unfold to see three evenly spaced crease marks along the quarter circle.

2. Fold a yellow print convex piece (Template B) in half diagonally, matching the points of the curve. Fold in half again and press creases in the seam allowance as in Step 1.

3. Pin the pieces together. Space pins about 1" apart when piecing precise curves. Place the yellow quarter circle on top of the white concave curve, matching the cen-ter marks of the two curves and aligning the edges at each crease. Pin the center of the curve. At the left side of the curve, align the straight edges and pin. Repeat for the right side. Next, pin the curves at the quarter marks. Finally, add four more pins in the remaining spaces.

4. Slowly sew along the curve, maintaining a scant ¼" seam allowance. I get the best results when I have the convex piece on the bottom and the larger concave piece on top, but the opposite works better for many people. Experiment to find what works best for you and your machine.

5. Examine the seam to make sure the seam allowance is consistent and that there are no puckers.

TIP

The "made-fabric" blocks will have areas that lie flat, and some areas with a bit of excess fabric. When cutting the shapes, the excess will release and the shapes can distort a bit. First do an initial rough cut, a second press, and a final cut to get precise results.

6. With corresponding white block pieces, repeat Steps 1 through 5 for the remaining yellow and orange convex and concave pieces to make a total of twenty-four 11½" × 11½" blocks.

ASSEMBLING THE QUILT

1. Arrange the blocks in four rows of six blocks each. **(Fig. 5)**

2. Sew the blocks into rows, matching and pinning seams where the curves meet. Press the seams in alternating directions.

3. Join the rows. Add the top and bottom white strips to complete the top.

4. Piece the backing to 74" × 93". Layer the backing, batting, and quilt top; baste and quilt as desired.

5. Piece the binding strips together with diagonal seams. Fold the binding in half, wrong sides together, and press. Bind the quilt with a ¼" seam allowance.

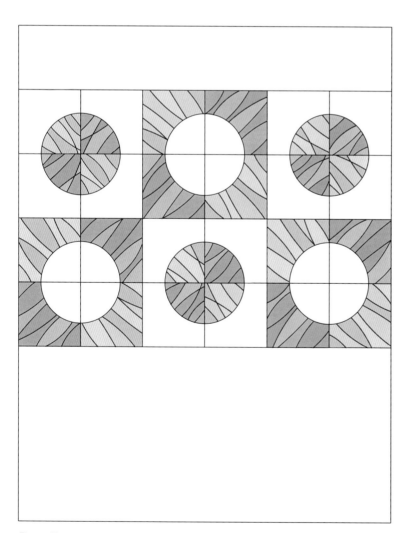

Figure 5

IMPROVISATIONAL PATCHWORK

A DESIGN WORKSHOP

Goal of the class: Encourage students to let go of learned habits and preconceived ideas about patchwork, and make discoveries about color, composition, and their own creativity.

TEACHER:
Denyse
Schmidt

Why Improvisational Patchwork?

Improvisationally pieced block.

Improvisation in any form—whether music, dance, comedy, or patchwork quilting—is about being in the moment and responding to what is happening now, rather than strictly adhering to a set pattern or script. I didn't invent improvisation as it applies to patchwork; it's been around as long as folks have been stitching together random bits and pieces of fabric, making do with worn-out clothing or whatever fabric is on hand to create an entirely new, useful, and beautiful object. The quilts that sparked my own interest in the craft were ones that showed evidence of this process, whether they were based on a traditional block pattern or were something completely unique.

The quilts I fell in love with were often quirky and odd, sometimes strikingly simple (and very modern-looking), often with unexpected and surprising fabric choices and combinations. These quilts were *not* about perfectly aligned seams or exquisitely crafted blocks. They were quilts that spoke about the joy and process of making, of the freedom of not having to get things "right," of being true and authentic— to the maker, their individual aesthetic and imagination, their abilities, and the materials and tools they had on hand. This doesn't mean that there isn't a foundation of skill and understanding with improvising, or even an underlying structure. In patchwork, the nature of the materials and the fact that you can sew only one piece to another at a time provides at least part of an inherent structure or system. As with any creative work, good structure is essential to the process, grounding the work so it can fly.

GETTING STARTED

In my Improvisational Patchwork class, proficiency in sewing is not required; the ability to remain open to new ideas and allow for exploration is. I love that the improv process is accessible to all, regardless of skill level. I've had students who had never used a sewing machine prior to my class, and they have made breathtaking work. Good craftsmanship is a skill acquired over time. A willingness to take chances, having the courage to go out on a limb and make "mistakes," is something we all innately possess, but we can cultivate and develop it. And it's really the only way we can learn anything new, to find our authentic voice.

Students attend my workshops for a lot of reasons. Some quilters have always used patterns and would like to learn a new way of working. Some folks feel they are stuck in a color rut, that everything they make looks the same. Other students see work that they would like to emulate, but they don't know how to get there. Many students want to loosen up, but they don't know where to start. Perhaps you fall into one of these categories. If we hang on fast to what we already know, we aren't able to make room for news ways of seeing things. Try working toward the mindset of a beginner: beginners have fewer preconceptions and expectations, and consequently feel they have less to lose by giving themselves over to the process with complete trust and freedom.

THREE BAGS AND A BLOCK

Pulling scraps randomly to create improv blocks.

When I first began teaching, I struggled to figure out a way to teach students something that, to me, felt entirely intuitive. I developed my Paper Bag technique to facilitate the process of letting go, allowing, and discovering. The intuitive part of choosing which color to use next or how to put it all together seemed to be the sticking point for many people. This technique evolved as a way to get people to experience the creative process without all the usual self-editing and second-guessing, and to learn to work around the desire to make things perfect, which seems to go hand-in-hand with having so many choices and options available to us in our modern world of plenty.

In the Paper Bag technique, you build each block one patch at a time. Sort scraps into paper bags roughly by size—small, medium, and large. The process is to blindly pull each piece out, one at a time, and sew it to the previous piece, or to the block, as it grows. The one-at-a-time part allows us to be in the present, not planning ahead or thinking about how things might turn out. Eliminating the element of choosing color and pattern alleviates the burden or need to make something "good" and helps us to notice the very elemental but important choices and decisions that remain.

It's always surprising to realize the number of decisions we routinely make in crafting something, without even being aware of it. Using whatever we draw from the bag, as it comes, and altering it as little as possible, connects us with the practice of "making do". The process facilitates juxtapositions—of varying colors, scale, print and solid—that we might not ordinarily have thought would work, and we are able see them in a nonjudgmental way, with fresh eyes.

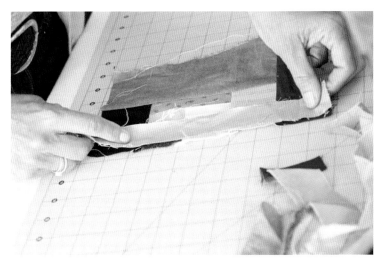

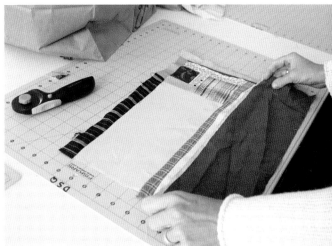

QUILTER —
TO QUILTER

Build a stash of random scraps—outside of your habitual choices or preferences—through online or in-person scrap swaps. This makes for a great sewing day with your guild if each member brings his or her own random scrap contributions, creating a wide-ranging selection of scraps for all to share.

Work quickly as you assemble your blocks and be strict with yourself about using the scraps you grab from the bag.

THE ELEMENT OF TIME

In any exercise or design problem, the setting of parameters is essential. In improvisational patchwork, time is a significant parameter. Sewing a quilt is a huge investment of time and energy, and this knowledge often triggers a strong desire for control in order to guarantee good (or familiar) results. The desire for predictable results is at odds with the nature of exploration and discovery, and of being in the moment. As a consequence, it's easy to get mired in overthinking. Here's where you need to let go. Use the element of time to stay focused on making and creating, not thinking or planning. The more you create, the more you have something to work with—to look at and respond to.

I give my students just twenty to thirty minutes to finish their first block (and less time for subsequent blocks). Set the time and simply dive in—there is no time to worry about the results. This timing exercise is about clearing the mental clutter of "it needs to look like this," and instead allows you to make discoveries and combinations you wouldn't have tried otherwise. In this way, you work toward discovering your own voice.

Students from Denyse's Beginning Improvisational Patchwork class.

Our most inspired ideas usually come in the *process* of making. It's similar to writing exercises: writing quickly and giving yourself permission to write badly. Usually in that rotten first draft (before the self-editor/critic pops up) there is the germ of an idea or a phrase that loosens up all the muscles and gets you *writing*. I am a big believer in learning viscerally. You can read about all kinds of theories and ideas, but until you actually make something, and see the work come through *your* hands, I don't think we ever really understand it, not on a gut level.

LOOK AT IT THIS WAY

One of the most important steps in improv piecing is to put up your work and look at it. The perspective of the work on the wall is very different from the blinders-on perspective of focusing on only one block at a time. A quilt by nature has many blocks, and seeing a block in the context of the whole can (and should) change how you see it.

After you complete a few timed blocks, put them up on your design wall and take a step back. Move things around. Move them around again.

Everyone has his or her own aesthetic preferences, so identifying what *you* are drawn to, what *you* like about something, and learning to articulate and understand *why* is the core of learning. Learning how to see, how to respond and find solutions, is the path to finding your own voice. It will be different for everyone.

QUILTER TO QUILTER

Remember to stand back and look at your work from the perspective of an entire quilt top. Try not to get hung up on making each block a work of art. Concentrate on the making, not planning and thinking, because it is in this process, when you aren't trying so hard, that you come up with ideas. Give yourself permission to produce without an end goal, and to make mistakes.

Step back and evaluate your work as you go.

Adding in focal fabrics.

ADDING IN CHOICES

In the second part of my workshop, I ask each student to bring one quarter yard of fabric from home. We prepare the fabric (see Quilter to Quilter at left) and incorporate it into the process—sometimes using the additional fabric, sometimes pulling scraps from the bag. The introduction of one small choice can change the game. Sometimes it throws people off and they revert to familiar habits. Experiment. Take it slowly and remember to always go back to the bags if you find you are second-guessing, planning ahead, or stuck in any way.

Even a single addition of fabric can add a great deal of complexity to the process. Really noticing and

understanding what happens to us when we have more options helps strengthen our awareness of all the choices we make in our work, all the time. With just one fabric of your choosing to add to the process, you now have questions to think about: *How often do I use it? Do I use the narrow strip now, or the wide or medium-size strip?* I suggest completing at least four blocks then put them up on the wall. What insight does this give you? Look at what happens when you use a lot of your chosen fabric, or just a little, and how that choice then informs the blocks as a group. Use those discoveries or that perspective to guide your choices as you continue to work.

QUILTER —— TO QUILTER

To add a focal fabric to the improv process, cut a fat quarter or quarter yard into strips that are narrow (1" or less), medium (1½" to 3"), and large (3" or wider). Put away the ruler and cut the strips freehand— a wobbly, thick-thin strip yields more variety. As you build your blocks, cut these strips to the length of the piece or block you are attaching it to.

Blocks don't have to be square. Play with a variety of sizes to invite new discoveries.

THE BIGGER PICTURE

Improvisational piecing is a creative process that will invariably get you thinking about patchwork, color, and composition in new ways. After experimenting with my Paper Bag technique, you can then incorporate what you have learned in a more structured way. You can continue to explore the wealth of discovery the process itself offers—it's possible to use the improvisational method as a way of making an entire quilt. If you love the colors of one of your Paper Bag blocks, use it to build a palette, making sure to add a range of hues and values of each color and adding in some unexpected oddball choices.

You can riff off the composition of an improvised block—repeating the essence of the composition, varying it each time (slightly and more dramatically), to create a repeating theme. Or you might compose a quilt top with just a strip or section of the improvised blocks, highlighting them in a designed way. Taking the accepted block form and thinking about ways you can change it up is another possibility for discovering a new way of quilt making. Scale is one element of design—juxtaposing small and large. An awareness of repetition, rhythm, and balance are other design elements that should be in your toolbox of possibilities when constructing your next quilt.

Whatever brings you to this process, use improvisational piecing as a laboratory where you can explore and experiment, and where the only failure is in not allowing yourself to fall flat on your face! You will surely make meaningful and valuable discoveries as you tap into the creative energy that is yours alone.

Explore and experiment.

THE ALTERNATE GRID

A PRACTICE WORKSHOP

Goal of the class: Reimagine how to piece together your blocks by exploring the variety of alternate setting styles modern quilters use. I'll teach you how to create quilt tops that seem complex, but rely on the same straightforward traditional construction methods. We'll explore modern twists on classic settings that start with the simplicity of variable framing and end with the more complex paneling technique.

TEACHER: Jacquie Gering

Design Without Limits

BREAKING OUT OF THE GRID

Modern quilters tend to view the quilt top much like a painter views a canvas: the elements of the design (the blocks or pieces) are placed wherever the quilter desires and, as a result, some modern quilters have found the traditional grid structure to be confining. Breaking out of the grid has allowed modern quilters to design without limits and explore and experiment with new setting possibilities.

In traditional quilts, the grid structure is fairly simple to identify. Students can see how the quilt was put together simply by looking at the quilt. In many modern quilts, however, the underlying structure of the quilt is more difficult to determine and in some cases totally disguised. Modern quilters desire options. We can choose to use traditional settings or explore alternatives. Enter the alternate grid, designing without limits.

TRADITIONAL SETTINGS

The Straight Set

Every quilt has an underlying structure, or setting. The most common setting in traditional quilts is the straight set, which is when the same size blocks are placed side by side to create an even grid of rows and columns **(Fig 1)**.

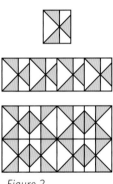

Figure 2

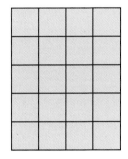

Figure 1

Most often, the same block is repeated throughout the grid. While the straight set is a fixed structure, there are many design options within that structure. Differently pieced blocks may be alternately placed within the grid, alternate blocks may be replaced with plain setting squares, or similar blocks can be rotated within the grid to create additional design possibilities. Stunning secondary designs may appear within the grid depending on the block designs **(Fig 2)**.

Sashing (plain or pieced strips) may be added between the blocks to further define the grid and frame the blocks. Cornerstones (squares placed where sashing strips meet) add complexity to a straight set **(Fig 3)**.

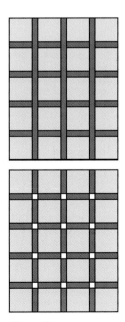

Figure 3

On-Point Setting

Another setting option common in traditional quilting is the on point setting. Setting a quilt on-point requires the blocks to be turned 45 degrees so that they sit on their corners. On-point quilt blocks are sewn in diagonal rows, leaving openings around the perimeter of the quilt, which are filled with corner and setting triangles **(Fig 4)**. On-point settings can add a special touch to an ordinary set of blocks.

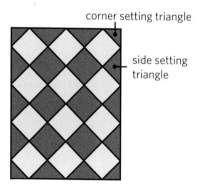

Figure 4

Medallion

Another classic setting in traditional quilts is the medallion. Medallion quilts typically have a large focal motif in the center of the quilt. The center medallion is then surrounded with one or more borders, each one often offering a different pieced pattern **(Fig 5)**. Medallion quilts are a wonderful setting to showcase complex appliqué or piecing.

Figure 5

MATH GEEK TIDBIT

The challenge of on point quilts is figuring the dimensions of setting and corner triangles. Lucky for us, there are foolproof formulas to calculate the dimensions for making setting and corner triangles for an on point set (Fig. 4).

CORNER SETTING TRIANGLES
(half-square triangles):

Finished size of block ÷ 1.414 + .875 = the cut size of the square. Squares are cut in half once diagonally to make corner setting triangles. Each square will yield two corner triangles.

SIDE SETTING TRIANGLES
(quarter-square triangles):

Finished size of block × 1.414 + 1.25 = the cut size of the square. Squares are cut in half twice diagonally (in an X) to make side setting triangles. Each square will yield four side triangles.

NOTE: Round all measurements to the nearest ⅛".

MODERN DESIGN INFLUENCES ON STRUCTURE

Breaking the grid allows for asymmetrical designs like the To the Point quilt.

Asymmetry

Modern design elements have influenced the variety of settings used in modern quilts. Modern quilters tend to love off-kilter and visually intriguing designs. Symmetry in quilts creates balance and a sense of elegance and formality. Asymmetry offers variety and can be quirky and stimulating. Altering the traditional grid supports the creation of asymmetrical designs.

Minimalism

Modern quilters tend to embrace simplicity and minimalism. Less is more. Simple shapes and fewer blocks are hallmarks of modern quilting. With fewer blocks, my students find that they have more options for where they might place them within their compositions. Working with fewer blocks allows us the flexibility to place blocks asymmetrically or anywhere we desire within the parameters of the quilt.

Negative Space

Negative space is the unoccupied area surrounding an object in a quilt, often referred to as "background." Negative space plays an important role in traditional quilts as the space within the piecing that defines the design. Modern

The Aftermath quilt with its bold shape placed thoughtfully without regard to the traditional grid.

quilters embrace the concept of negative space and typically incorporate more negative space in their original compositions than their traditional counterparts.

Modern quilters use negative space to simplify designs (see the Large-Scale Piecing workshop on page 124, which discusses one way to achieve simplicity using negative space) to draw attention to the focal point of a quilt, or to create interesting shapes within the background.

I encourage you to alter the grid to allow the negative space to flow in, around, and between your quilt blocks. Altering the traditional grid allows modern quilters flexibility to utilize negative space as a powerful design tool.

The Deconstructed Nine-Patch quilt is a wonderful example of an imaginative use of negative space. The black background surrounds and flows in and out of the nine patch medallion.

Scandia Crush uses variable framing.

ALTERNATE GRID STRUCTURES

One of the advantages of the traditional grid structure, especially the straight set, is that it is simple to understand and easy to construct. The term "alternate grid" can create a vision of complex construction, but I assure you that most alternate grid settings are also simple to create and require only small tweaks to the traditional grid. Some alternate settings actually maintain the grid structure while at the same time create the illusion that there is no grid.

Variable Framing

A simple way of creating the illusion of no grid is to use variable framing to allow either same-size or variable-size blocks to "float" randomly within the negative space. The minimalist log cabin blocks in *Scandia Crush* (pictured left) are variably framed.

To use variable framing, decide on the finished size of the blocks for the quilt, for example, 20½". Using the example below, make six blocks in varying sizes at least 4" smaller than the finished size. Blocks could range from very small, for example 6" × 6", to as large as 16" × 16". Then bring each of the six blocks to the finished size using framing strips of the same background fabric. The key to making variable framing look modern is to alter the size of the framing strips for each block.

Tape out the finished block size on your design wall and place the block within the taped frame. Where you place the block within the frame will determine where the block "floats" in the negative space. Once the block is placed, measure from the top of the block to the tape (from point A to point B in **Figure 1** and add ½" to account for the seam allowance; that measurement will determine the width of the framing strip to add to the top of the block. The length of the framing strip will be the length of the block. Repeat this process for all four sides of the block.

Once all the blocks for the quilt have been variably framed, they can be arranged and sewn together as a straight set **(Fig. 2)**,

sewing the blocks together to form rows and then sewing the rows together to complete the quilt top. Even though this is a traditional straight setting, it will appear that the blocks are floating randomly within the negative space **(Fig. 3)**.

Figure 1

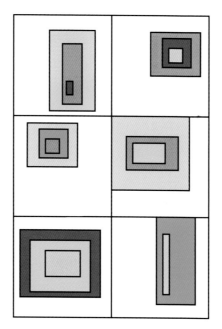

Figure 2

Figure 3

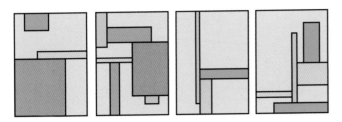

Figure 4

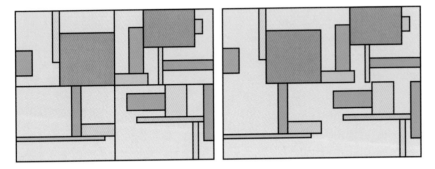

Figure 5

The Offset Grid

A simple way to vary the setting of their quilt and still maintain simple construction of rows or columns is to offset the blocks by moving them up or down a certain distance. The *Burst* quilt I designed for this workshop is an example of using the offset grid. Notice how the *Burst* block design changes and creates various secondary designs depending simply upon the amount of offsetting.

burst block

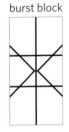

straight set

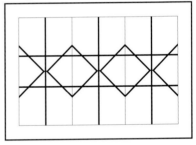

Offsetting blocks that are traditionally set in an aligned position creates new design possibilities and a modern look. See what happens when simple half-square triangle blocks are slid into an offset position (see right).

When blocks are in an offset setting, there will be spaces to fill at the top and bottom of columns or on the sides of rows. These can be filled with partial blocks or with background fabric. Slide your blocks up, down, or over and see what happens.

Inflow

Another way to achieve an alternate grid look while maintaining the traditional grid construction is to allow the negative space to flow in and out of your blocks. This is accomplished by making blocks that have background fabric that is interspersed with the prints or solids within the block. The inflow setting is perfect for improvisationally pieced blocks. Look at these blocks in **Figure 4.**

Notice how pieces of background fabric are placed within the block. There is background fabric both on the edges of the blocks and within the blocks. Notice what happens when these blocks are placed together in a traditional straight set **(Fig. 5).**

The block structure seems to disappear. Since each block is the same size, they can be pieced together using traditional grid construction. The background fabric flowing in, out, and through the blocks creates the illusion that the traditional grid is absent.

offset options

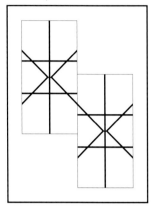 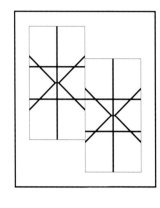 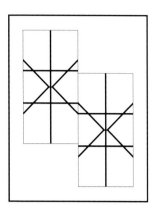

Simple offsetting of a block creates multiple design options.

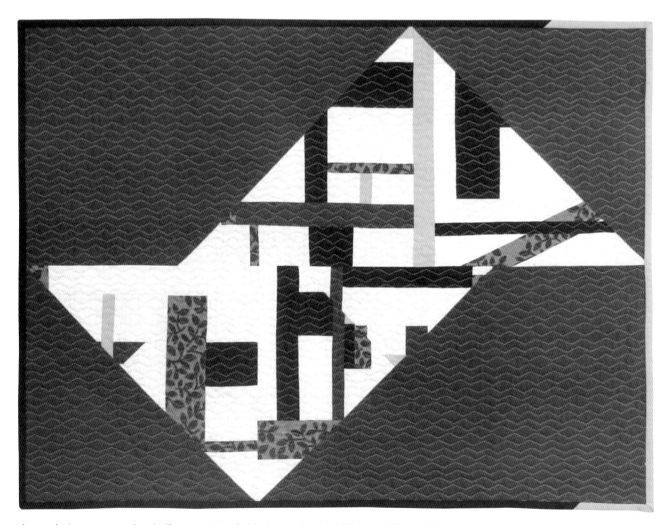

A new design appears when half square triangle blocks are simply slid into an offset position.

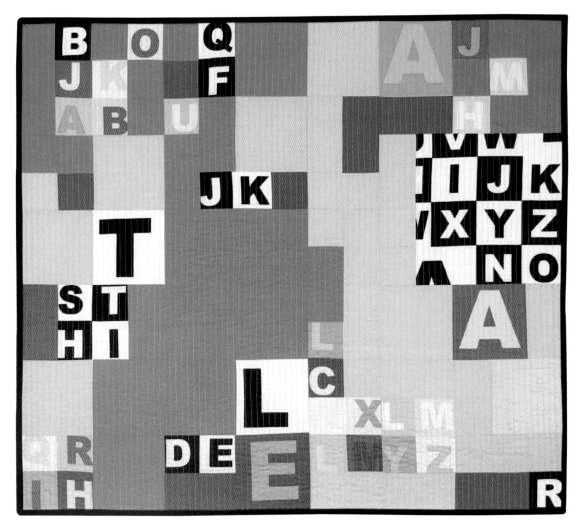

Quilt made with magic number blocks.

Magic Numbers

Many modern quilters like to use different size blocks in their quilts. There is a structure that supports doing that, called "paneling," perhaps the most free-wheeling setting (see page 74). If you're not quite ready for that, then the concept of "magic numbers" might be for you. The magic is in making block sizes that will fit together automatically, which allows for flexibility in creating a design and still provides simple construction. For example, blocks with the finished sizes of 2", 4", and 8" will fit together beautifully and can work with both square and rectangular-shaped blocks. 2", 4" and 6" blocks will also fit together magically. These are only two of the possible magic number combinations. I'm sure you can find even more.

Magic number quilts are constructed like simple puzzles remembering that squares and rectangles are your friends. In the example on the right, you can see how blocks 1 – 4 form section one and blocks 5 – 9 form section two. Sew the two sections together to form the block.

This magic number (above) quilt was made with 2", 4" and 8" finished blocks. Integrating blocks made from two background fabrics leads to an even more modern look where the blocks appear to float in the negative space with no discernible underlying structure.

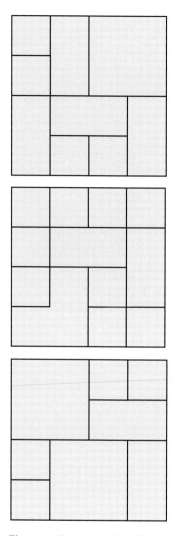

These are three examples of how magic number blocks might be put together to form different designs.

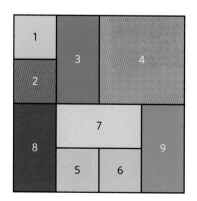

The numbers show the sewing order of these magic number blocks.

In the Broken Cogs quilt the cogs are pieced and then hand appliqued to the background.

Appliqué

Not much needs to be said about the alternate grid possibilities of appliqué. Because appliqué can be placed anywhere on a quilt top, if you desire no limits in quilt structure, and you want to incorporate large areas of negative space, hand or machine appliqué may be the way to go. See the Circles and Curves workshop on page 82, which presents many different appliqué techniques. The Broken Cogs quilt is a great example of creating a unique quilt setting with appliqué. With applique the sky is the limit!

The Modern Medallion

Many modern quilters love to showcase one or a few blocks, and the medallion setting is designed to do just that. Some prefer to go with a traditional centered medallion with one or more surrounding

The Bursting with Pride quilt is a four-block medallion quilt with the blocks set on point.

borders, but that's not the limit to the medallion setting. With modern quilters' love of asymmetry, the medallion setting is the perfect opportunity to place the medallion or cluster of blocks off-center. Creating an off-center medallion is as easy as creating the center block or cluster of blocks, placing that block where desired within the parameter of the quilt, and filling in the remaining space in the top with background fabric. The construction process is the same as variable framing, but on a larger scale.

Paneling

The final option for creating an alternate grid structure is paneling. Paneling can be used to create an underlying structure that tricks the eye and in many cases disguises the grid completely. Panels can be thought of as different size sections that will fit together seamlessly to create the underlying structure of a quilt. The first step in paneling is to define the parameters of the quilt. One way to do this is to tape out the outside edge of the quilt with painter's tape onto a design wall. If a quilt is going to be large, this can

be done in several sections instead of one large rectangle. The panels (sections) within the parameters of the quilt can be created before you place the blocks where you want them, or you can create the panels after the blocks are placed and then adjust any placement to make sure you can create panels that will be easy to construct. Most of my students find it easier to design the panels first and then place their blocks. **Figure 3** shows an example of a simple five-paneled structure.

Here's how it works. The number one rule in paneling is to understand that squares and rectangles are your friends. Panels within a quilt top can be different sizes as long as they come together to form squares and rectangles that can be sewn together easily without partial seams. After you have defined the panels within the quilt top, place the blocks within the panels to create the look you desire.

Once the blocks are placed, the next step is to add background fabric around the blocks to create the panels. Measure from the edge of the block to the taped boundary of the panel and add ½" (or a bit extra) for seam allowance, then cut the strip that width to extend the block to the edge of the panel. Repeat this process to fill in all the background area around the

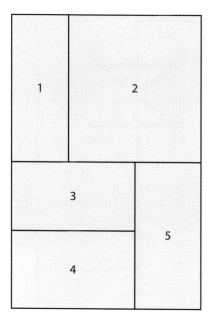

Figure 3

block. Placing a block on the edge of the panel (see panel 3 in **Figure 4**) makes this process easier since you only have to measure and extend two sides of the block. Square the panel to the predetermined size after all of the background fabric is added.

When the panels are complete, sew the panels together like a puzzle. In the panel structure in **Figure 4**, the panels would be sewn in the following order: Panel 1 to panel 2, panel 3 to panel 4, panel 3/4 to panel 5, and finally panel 1/2 to panel 3/4. Paneled structures can be as simple as the example in **Figure 4** or they can be more intricate, just so long as the panels ultimately come together to form squares and rectangles that can be sewn together easily. You are not limited to placing just one block

per panel. Multiple blocks can be placed within a panel and the same principles of paneling apply. Notice how sub-panels are created within the single panel **(Fig. 5)**. Again, remember that squares and rectangles are our friends and all of the sub-panels will come together easily.

Paneling can be used to create complex underlying structures for modern quilts. Paneled settings can create varying looks for your quilts depending on the type of blocks that are set into the panels. Static blocks (blocks with a definitive design such as pinwheels or stars) will float or cluster within the quilt top, but will still maintain the look of blocks within the overall structure. Blocks with inflow of background fabric, especially those pieced improvisationally, will blend into the background making the underlying structure less distinguishable. You can try this paneling technique yourself using blocks you created using the process taught in the Improvisational Patchwork workshop on page 52.

Creating modern quilts is all about pushing limits and rethinking how a quilt can come together. These alternative grid options are only a starting point for how modern quilters are reimagining quilt structure and how you can, too. Embrace the alternative grid and make your quilt your own way.

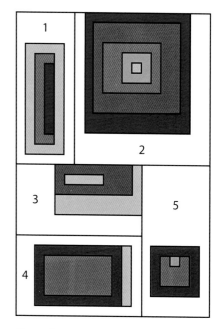

Figure 4

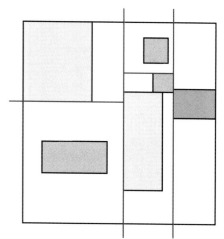

Figure 5

CUTTING THE FABRIC

1. From the white fabric, cut the following:

☐ Three 20" strips. From these, cut twelve 10" × 20" A rectangles.

☐ Three 5" strips. From these, cut twelve 5" × 10" B rectangles.

☐ Three 5½" strips. From these, cut six 5½" × 18½" C rectangles.

☐ Three 19½" strips. From these, cut two 19½" × 14" D rectangles, one 19½" × 25" E rectangle, one 19½" × 21" F rectangle, one 19½" × 7" G rectangle.

2. From the black fabric, cut eighteen 1" strips.

3. From these, cut the following:

☐ Twelve 1" × 20" E strips.

☐ Twelve 1" × 16" F strips.

☐ Twelve 1" × 10" G strips.

☐ Twelve 1" × 9" H strips.

4. From the binding fabric, cut eight 2¼" strips.

MAKING THE BLOCKS

Block 1

1. Sew a black E strip between two white A rectangles as shown. Press. Repeat with remaining A rectangles to make a total of six units.

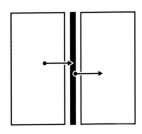

2. Cut the block horizontally from edge to edge 6" from the top to create two sections. Sew an E strip between the two sections, matching the top and bottom black strip intersection. Press.

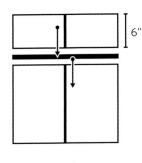

Parallel pin and test to get perfect matches.

3. With the block placed as shown below, make a mark on the right and left edge of the fabric 10" down from the top.

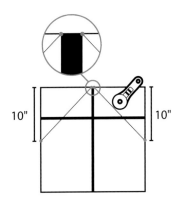

10"   10"

4. Slice the fabric from the mark on the right side to the top right corner of the black strip. Repeat for the left side, slicing from the mark on the left side of the block to the top left corner of the black strip.

5. Sew a black F strip to the right side cut edge, allowing the strip to extend past both ends. Press.

6. Sew the right section to the black strip, matching the intersection exactly. Press. Trim the top of the block back to a straight edge.

7. Repeat Steps 5 and 6 for the left side of the block.

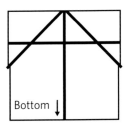

Bottom ↓

8. Repeat Steps 1 through 7 to complete six Block 1 blocks.

9. Trim the bottom of the blocks so that the height measures 19½". Trim both sides so that the blocks measure 19½" × 19½".

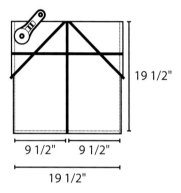

Block 2

Block 2 follows the same construction steps as Block 1, but with different measurements.

1. Sew a black G strip between two white B rectangles. Press. Repeat for all twelve B rectangles to make a total of six units.

2. With the black strip orientated vertically, cut the block from Step 1 with the strip oriented vertically. Cut the block horizontally from edge to edge 3" from the top to create two sections. Sew a black G strip between the two sections, matching the intersection. Press.

3. Referencing Step 3 from Block 1, make a mark on the right and left edges of the fabric this time 5" down from the top of the block.

4. Slice the fabric from the mark on the right side of the block to the top right corner of the black strip. Press. Repeat for the left side, slicing from the mark on the left side of the block to the top left corner of the black strip.

5. Sew a strip to the right side cut edge, allowing the strip to extend past both ends.

6. Sew the right section to the black strip, matching the intersection exactly. Press. Trim the top of the block back to a straight edge.

7. Repeat Steps 5 and 6 for the left side of the block.

8. Repeat Steps 1 through 7 to complete six Block 2 blocks.

9. Trim both bottom of the blocks so that height measures 9½". Trim the sides so that the blocks measure 9½" × 9½".

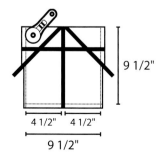

QUILTER TO QUILTER

Matching Tip:
To achieve perfect matches, at the site of the match, place pins parallel to the edge of the fabric directly on the ¼" seam line as shown. Test by flipping the fabric back to the right side to view the match. Adjust, re-pin, and retest as needed before you start to sew.

ASSEMBLING THE QUILT

1. Sew two Block 1 blocks together as shown. Press the seam open. Repeat to make three large blocks.

large block

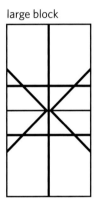

2. Sew two Block 2 blocks together as shown. Press the seam open. Sew one C rectangle to each side. Repeat to make three small blocks.

small block

3. Place the large and small blocks and the D, E, F, and G rectangles as shown in at right. Note that the D, E, F, and G rectangles are larger than necessary to allow for flexibility of matching up seams when the three columns are attached.

4. Sew the blocks in columns from top to bottom, matching the intersections between the large and small blocks.

5. Sew the columns together, matching the intersection of the large blocks. (See the circled areas on the Construction Diagram at right).

6. Trim to even the top and bottom edges of the quilt. The quilt top measures 57½" × 81".

FINISHING THE QUILT

1. Piece the backing to 65" × 89". Layer backing, batting, and quilt top; baste and quilt as desired. Trim the backing and batting.

2. Join the binding strips with diagonal seams. Fold the binding strip, wrong sides together, and press. Bind the quilt using a ¼" seam allowance.

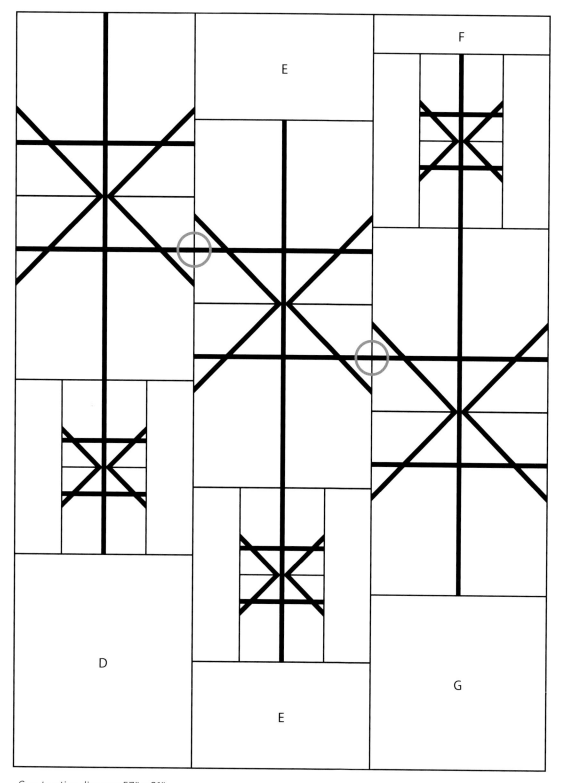

Construction diagram 57" x 81".

CIRCLES AND CURVES

A PRACTICE WORKSHOP

Goal of the class: Take the fear out of working with curves and circles. Go through each of these techniques with me and you will see how easy it is to achieve perfect piecing using a variety of styles. You are sure to find the technique you prefer that will keep you from shying away from patterns that have curves and even to begin incorporating them into designs of your own.

TEACHER:
Cheryl Arkison

Circles and Curves

A compass will come in very handy.

QUILTER TO QUILTER

To find the center of a circle when you've traced a round object, try this little trick. After cutting out your circle, fold it in half, then in half again so that it looks like quarter circles. Unfold the circle; the intersection of the fold lines is you center point.

CIRCLE GEOMETRY

Don't run away, but we need a tiny math lesson before launching into the piecing fun. Take a few minutes to get these geometry concepts down, and your circle creations will be even easier.

There are two easy ways to accurately draw a circle.

1. Find a round object and trace it. Bowls, plates, cups, lids, and more work wonderfully. Your kitchen probably has the best selection.

2. Grab an elementary school geometry set (or raid your kid's school supplies) and release the compass! This tool allows you to easily draw a circle to a precise diameter.

There are a lot of notions and rulers available to the quilter as well. I'm not a big fan of extra bits and bobs in my sewing space so I tend to stick with the basics, but if you love having a lot of supplies, then explore the many circle creation options available at your favorite local or online quilt shop.

Whatever method you use for drawing a circle, I always remind my students to use a sharp pencil or fine-tip pen. This is not the time for a thick line or marker.

CUTTING PAPER TEMPLATES

When cutting your paper template for the circle, you need to make long cuts. Open your scissors wide, start the cut as close to the joint of the scissor blades as possible. Then move your paper, not your scissors, as you slowly close the blades to make the cut. Before the scissor tips close completely, open the blades wide again and repeat. Short snips, made with the tips of the scissors, cause jagged edges. Long cuts give you a smoother edge.

Perhaps most important, make sure you keep a dedicated pair of paper scissors handy. Do not use your fabric scissors when cutting out paper templates!

Keep the scissors open very large and move the paper, not the scissors.

CIRCLE TERMINOLOGY

Circles all start with a point. The center point of the circle is the key for accurate measurement and drawing. Even if you simply trace a bowl to draw your circle, it is helpful to know where your center is.

From the center point you can accurately draw your circle. Tracing an object is wonderful, but it doesn't give you precise control over the size of the finished piece.

DIAMETER

The width of your circle. When I refer to how large a circle is, I am referring to the diameter of the circle.

RADIUS

Half of the diameter, or the measurement from the center point to the edge of the circle. This term is especially important to keep in mind when measuring quarter circles.

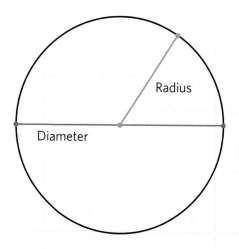

FABRIC SELECTION TIPS

When it comes to fabric selection for your appliqué and inset circle projects, it isn't quite the case that "anything goes."

Be sure to create a defined boundary between the circle and the background fabric. Without effective contrast, you merely have a wavy line. (see the Principles of Color workshop on page 6 to learn more about creating contrast).

Watch out for:

- Background color on your circle fabric that is the same as on your background fabric.

- Bleeding stripes, where one particular stripe gets lost when paired with a background fabric that coordinates too well.

- Blending the patterns (a print with a white pattern, for example), can get lost on a white background square.

- Don't hesitate to use low contrasting fabrics, but take note of the different design possibilities when you do so.

Featuring fabrics:

- Take advantage of 5" and 10" pre-cuts for making circles.

- Both large-scale and small-scale prints work for circles and curves. Mix them up in one project for tremendous impact.

- Try fussy cutting favorite prints and put them on display in a circle.

- Fabrics that include arcs or circles, such as paisleys, dots, or sweeping florals, can add movement.

- Sripes are great in circles. Vary the angle of the stripes on the finished block for extra elements in your design.

Background fabrics:

Always check that your background fabric does not show through the circle, particularly when working with appliqué circles. If necessary, cut away the background fabric behind the circle. This eliminates both the bulk of two layers and addresses any transparency issues. To do this, pinch the circle fabric in one hand and the background in the other. Pull apart. Using scissors, cut away the excess fabric of the background fabric. I like to make these cuts as close to the seam allowance as possible, while still keeping a reasonable ¼", so that the piece I cut away is a more usable scrap.

APPLIQUÉ CIRCLES

Over the years I've tried many appliqué methods. These include using aluminum foil and cardboard templates or sewing fabric to a dryer sheets or lightweight interfacing. These techniques have given me inconsistent or bulky results. My favorite method for making perfect circles uses freezer paper, a hot iron, and a basting or gathering stitch.

1. Make the Circle

Determine the circle's diameter. Remember, if you aren't concerned with making a specific size, go ahead and trace an object that is more or less the size you want. Draw your circle on the dull side of the freezer paper **(Fig. 1)**. Cut it out with paper scissors.

2. Apply the Template

Pick your fabric for the circle. With an iron, press the freezer paper circle – shiny side down – to the wrong side of your fabric. Leave enough extra fabric for a ½" seam allowance. Cut your fabric around the circle, remembering to leave that seam allowance **(Fig. 2)**.

3. Gather the Edges

Set your sewing machine stitch length for a straight stitch to the longest it can go— likely a 5 or 6. Leaving long tails of thread, slowly stitch around the circle, approxi-

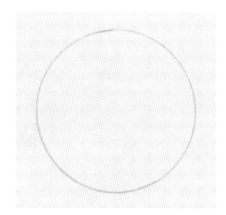

Figure 1

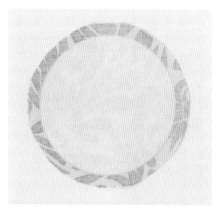

Figure 2

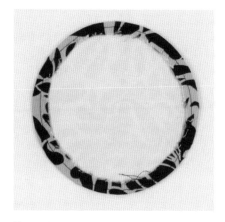

Figure 3

Figure 4

QUILTER TO QUILTER

Even the best of us end up with points when we gather. Keep a stiletto or seam ripper handy to open up the folds that create the point. It is easier if you catch these at the ironing board rather than the sewing machine. Points are more likely to happen on smaller circles, so I tend to shorten my basting stitch to a 4 or 5 on the smaller circles, reducing the potential for points.

mately ⅜" from the edge of the freezer paper template. When you get to the end, stitch slightly to the side of where you started and go three or four stitches beyond. You want to overlap, but not to stitch over where you started.

Holding the circle down on a flat surface, pull the bobbin threads to gently gather the fabric around the edge of the template **(Fig. 3)**. It won't go evenly at first and you may need to ease the gather around the template. Take care that the template edge does not get folded over. Once your fabric is gathered, press the circle well from the front and back. Remove the freezer paper (reserving for use five or six more times) and press again.

4. Attach to Background

Attach the circle to the background fabric **(Fig. 4)** using one of the techniques discussed next (see page 88).

Attaching the Circle

First consider your thread. Go for high contrast to emphasize the circle edges or a matching thread for subtlety.

The Straight Stitch

Set your machine to your basic stitch and stitch along the edge of the circle as close to the edge as you feel confident being sure to secure the seam allowance underneath **(Fig. 1)**. I recommend using a clear foot if you have one so that it is easier to see your stitching.

The Zigzag Stitch

Use an invisible thread, a clear zigzag foot if you have one, and set the stitch length wider to tack down the edges, catching the circle and the background alternately with each stitch or entirely on the circle depending on the look you like **(Fig. 2)**.

Machine Appliqué

Some machines have options for a machine appliqué or blanket stitch **(Fig. 3)**. If you set your stitch width to be quite narrow and use a coordinating or invisible thread, the stitching should be very subtle. This is a great option whether you are planning an allover quilting design or something that makes the circle pop. Again, use a clear foot if you have one so that you can really see your stitching.

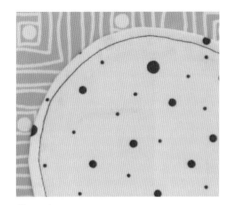

Figure 1

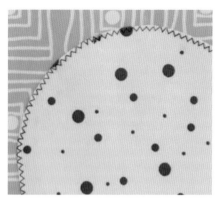

Figure 2

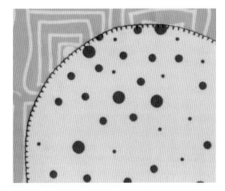

Figure 3

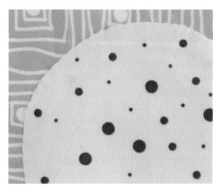

Figure 4

Hand Appliqué

Circles are a great option for hand work. You can make up a few circles and background pieces and carry them with you for hand sewing. Use your basic hand appliqué stitch to sew down your circles **(Fig. 4)**.

There are times when you want your piecing to be more subtle. Reverse circles achieve the look of an inset circle (see page 89)— with no visible stitching and the circle seemingly pieced into the background—without the stress and potential stretching of the block.

(see page 89)

TIP

Here is an easy trick for making sure your circles are placed in the center of your block. Fold the background block in half, then in half again so the block is defined in quarters. Finger press so the edges are evident. Do the same thing with the circle. To place the circle in the exact center of the block, line up the edges of each fold on the circle with those on the background piece. Pin in place.

REVERSE CIRCLES

1. Create the Template

Cut a piece of freezer paper to the size of the unfinished block. Mark the center of your freezer paper square **(Fig. 1)**. From that point measure out the desired radius of your circle and use your compass to draw the circle.

Cut out the circle from the freezer paper. This gives you a freezer paper square with a circle missing from the center.

2. Prepare the Background

Press the shiny side of the freezer paper template to the wrong side of your background fabric. Cut out a background square directly along the lines of your template **(Fig. 2)**.

Make a snip in your background fabric ½" from the edge of the circle, where there is no freezer paper. Cut around the circle, leaving a ½" seam allowance **(Fig. 3)**.

Snip a fringe in the seam allowance of the circle using only the tips of your scissors. *Stop just shy of the edge.* Make a cut every ½", closer together if your circle is smaller than 6".

Once you've created a cut fringe all the way around, press it over the edge of the circle. A hot iron, a little starch, and a careful hand

leaves you with a fringe folded over the edge of the freezer paper template **(Fig. 4)**.

3. Apply the Circle

Cut out a square of your circle fabric one inch wider than the diameter of the circle in your prepared background. Press flat.

On the right side of the background fabric wrapped around the freezer paper **(Fig. 4)**, dab a dot of fabric glue on each individual

fringe. Take care not to get glue on the freezer paper.

Attaching the circle fabric is easier to do one half at a time to reduce stretch. Fold your circle fabric square in half with the wrong sides together. Place the right side of the circle fabric square against the glued fringe of the background fabric wrapped around the freezer paper. Press down to secure, moving from the center to the edge of the circle, without pulling

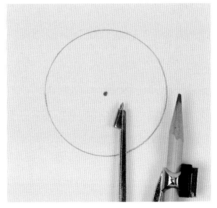

Figure 1

Figure 2

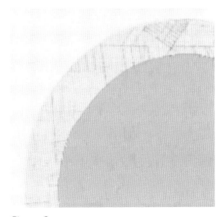

Figure 3

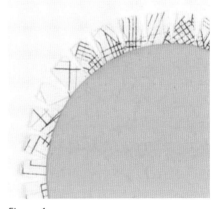

Figure 4

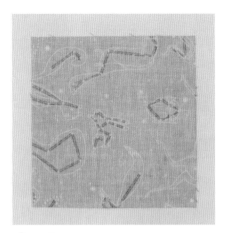

Figure 5

Figure 6

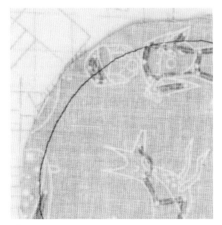

Figure 7

or stretching. Unfold the circle fabric and press down on the second half of the circle **(Fig. 5)**.

Flip the block over and, tuck in anyerrant bits of fringe that may have popped to the front. Press to seal the glue. Trim the excess circle fabric either before or after stitching, whichever you are most comfortable with.

4. Sew the Circle Fabric in Place

Shorten your sewing machine stitch slightly, to a 2. Place your block with the background fabric on the top. Carefully remove the freezer paper. Gather the background fabric toward the center.

Insert your needle on the fold line from the edge of the circle **(Fig. 6)**. You are sewing overtop the fringe glued to the circle fabric. Slowly, sew all the way around the circle.

Press the block from the front. Press and lift the iron to avoid distortion. **(Fig. 7)**.

QUILTER TO QUILTER

If the lighting in your sewing space isn't great or you need an extra guide for sewing, trace the edge of the circle with a pencil before you cut the fringe.

INSET CURVES

When you want a portion of a circle, such as a quarter or a half, use the inset technique.

1. Templates

My personal preference is for freezer paper templates. That way you can make a curve in any size. *Whatever the template, make sure you cut your fabric with seam allowances.*

If accuracy is important in your block, use your compass when drawing these partial curves.

Decide on the size of the block and inset curve that you want. I've used a 6" finished block with a 4" finished quarter circle for our example.

Draw a 6" square. From one corner measure out 4" and mark. Use your compass to draw a curve with the point of the compass in the corner. Start at your 4" mark and let the compass draw the curve. Label the inside of the curve A and the outside B **(Fig. 1)**. Then cut out the two pieces.

We will be adding seam allowances when we cut the fabric. If you prefer, you can add the seam allowance to your template.

2. Cut and Prepare Fabric Pieces

Press your fabric well to remove any creases. Apply the shiny side

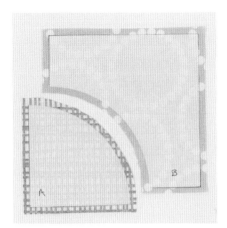

Figure 1

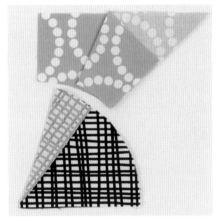

Figure 2

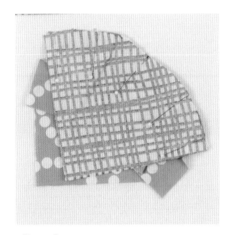

Figure 3

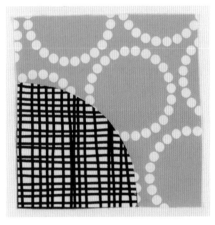

Figure 4

of the freezer paper template to the wrong side of the fabric.

With a fabric marking pen add a seam allowance to each piece or, if you are comfortable enough, eyeball the ¼" addition. Cut around both templates **(Fig. 1)**. If you added the seam allowance to your templates first, cut your fabric on the template edge.

Apply registration marks along each of the curves to ensure accuracy. Start with A. Fold it in half, lining up the straight sides. Finger

press the fold. If fabric is busy, you will want to mark a dot on the fold, at the edge. Unfold, then fold the sides in to the middle. Finger press and mark if necessary. Repeat with piece B. This marks your piece in quarters **(Fig. 2)**.

3. Pin, Sew, and Press

Using your registration marks/creases as guides, pin together A and B, wrong sides together. Pin the center mark first, then pin the ends. Finally, pin the quarter marks.

With the background piece (B) on the bottom, stitch around the curve backstitching at the beginning and end. Focus only on the stitches between where you are at the moment and the next pin. Hold the pieces at the next pin, taut but not stretched **(Fig. 3)**. When you reach the pin remove it and repeat.

There is no need to clip the seams. Press, do not iron, to avoid distorting the block. The seam allowance can be pressed toward the background or the curve **(Fig. 4)**.

MAKE IT IMPROVISATIONALLY

Check out the Improvisational Patchwork workshop on page 52.
In this workshop, the instructor talks about working in the moment to
create blocks. Curves can be given that improv treatment as well.

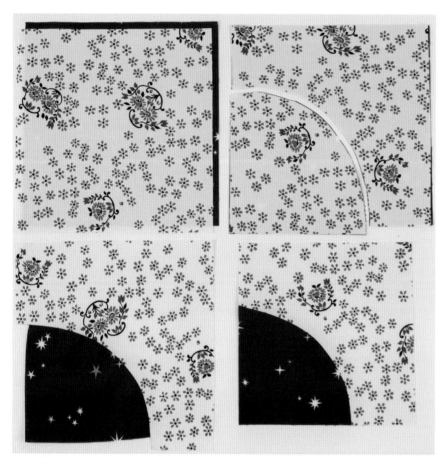

Steps for making improve quarter circles.

Improv Quarter Circles

Making quarter circles freehand is
a great improv technique.

Cut two pieces of fabric, roughly
1 inch larger than the finished
block size you hope to trim your
block to.

Layer your background fabric and
circle fabric, right sides up. Cut a
rough quarter circle through both
pieces. Without pinning or making any registration marks, loosely
hold together the pieces, wrong
sides together, at the center. Don't
worry about the pieces lining

QUILTER — TO QUILTER

If you have an even feed
foot or walking foot on
your machine, curves
tend to move through
the machine with very
little guidance. If you
have to, stop and
reposition the fabric
in the needle down
position to make small
adjustments. Making big
adjustments will result
in points and puckers
in your finished curve.

up – this is improv! Keeping the
inside of the curved piece on the
top, slowly sew the two pieces
together, stopping to line up the
edge just in front of you every few
stitches.

When you are finished, it won't
look like much. Press the block and
square it up. You do have to cut
off quite a bit to get it square,
which is why you start with pieces
at least 1" larger than you hope to
finish with.

Examples of a variety of curvy shapes you can create.

QUILTER TO QUILTER

Fabric glue is available at most quilt and craft stores. In a pinch, you can use regular white glue or a glue stick. Be careful not to overload the fabric with glue and it will all wash out.

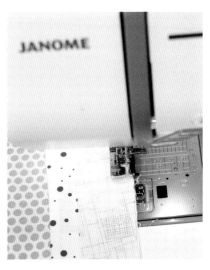

Sewing gradual curve strips.

Curved Appliqué Shapes

There is nothing stopping you from creating curved shapes. Adjusting the curve can require a little more finesse when gathering, so take it slowly. If there are points in your shape, a fold may be required to get the edge lay flat. On a concave curve (say, on a kidney shape) a little clip in the seam allowance is needed.

Gradual Curves

Not all curves have to look like they just stepped out of a circle. Long and gradual curves are easily made. They add movement and take the concept of a strip to a new level.

Cut curves into your strips with a rotary cutter or scissors. Then line up the edges and sew. When you go to press, it becomes clear that things don't want to play nicely and lay flat. That's okay. Press the seams anyway, using steam or starch.

When you begin with a piece slightly larger than your finished block size you can always square up. Once squared and eventually quilted, the unevenness disappears.

Sewing curves this way definitely requires a gentle hand. And the curve must be gradual, like the slope of cursive writing. Strong curves should be sewn with one of the other techniques discussed earlier in the chapter.

COMPOSE YOURSELF

I have a favorite piece of fabric made by Alexander Henry. It is a seemingly random pattern of black shapes on a cream background. That's it. I've used it so many times that I only have snippets of it left. The design for this quilt was inspired by that fabric. It is my attempt to record it just one more time before the scraps disappear forever.

To make this quilt your own, take the blocks and shake up the layout. There is no reason to stick with what I've done. You could also take the techniques learned here or from another workshop in the book and design your own blocks. Size them up or down by adding or removing blocks and adjusting the border/amount of negative space. Have fun and create your own design.

FINISHED QUILT SIZE: 72" × 72"
FINISHED BLOCK SIZE: 12" × 12"

MATERIALS

4 yards of background fabric

1 yard of feature fabric

4½ yards of backing fabric

⅔ yard of binding fabric

80" × 80" batting

Freezer paper, compass, and pencil

CUTTING THE FABRIC

1. From the background fabric, cut seven 12½" border strips.

2. From the remainder of the background fabric and beginning with the longest 2½ strip first, cut the following strips and subcut the number of pieces listed in the table below. The letters in parentheses correspond to the diagram labels in each individual block illustration.

3. From the feature fabric, cut the following strips and subcut the number of pieces listed in the table below. The letters in parentheses correspond to the diagram labels.

Background Fabric Strips	Subcuts					
	2½"	4½"	5½"	6½"	8½"	12½"
Four 1½" strips	3 (A)	5 (B)		2 (C)	4 (D)	5 (E)
Five 2½" strips	4 (F)	1 (G)	2 (H)	3 (I)	3 (J)	9 (K)
One 3½" strip						1 (L)
Four 4½" strips		2 (M)			5 (N)	7 (O)
One 5½" strip			4 (P)			1 (Q)
Two 6½" strip		1 (R)		3 (S)	1 (T)	1 (U)
One 12½" strip						3 (V)

Feature Fabric Strips	Subcuts					
	2½"	3" square	4½"	6½"	8½"	12½"
One 1 ½" strip			3 (W)	2 (X)		
Two 2 ½" strips	7 (Y)				2 (Z)	3 (AA)
Three 4 ½" strips			6 (BB)		5 (CC)	2 (DD)
From the remaining feature fabric, cut three 3" squares (EE), one 5 ½" square (FF), two 7" squares (GG), two 9" squares (HH), and one 8 ½" × 10 ½" rectangle (II).						

MAKE IT SCRAPPY THE FABRIC

If you want to make this quilt using scraps, as I did, simply decide which fabrics you want to include in each block, make a list of the letters from 'W' onward, and use the chart above for your cutting list.

Construction diagram 72" x 72".

MAKING THE BLOCKS

Block 1

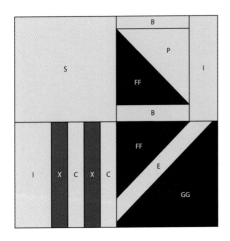

1. Cut one 5" × 5" feature fabric square (FF) and one 7" × 7" feature fabric square (GG) in half on the diagonal. Place one large feature fabric triangle in your scrap basket.

2. Sew one 1½" × 12½" background strip (E) on the diagonal edge of one large triangle with overhang on each end. Sew one small triangle to the other side of the strip, lining up with the corners of the large triangle. Press and trim to 6½" × 6½". This is Unit A.

3. Trim one 5½" × 5½" background square (P) to 5" × 5"; cut once on the diagonal to make two triangles. Place one triangle in the scrap basket.

4. Sew the background triangle to the remaining small feature fabric triangle. Press and trim to 4 ½" × 4 ½". Sew one 1½" × 4½" back-ground fabric rectangle (B) to the top and bottom. Press. Sew one 2½" × 6½" background rectangle (I) to the right side. Press. This is Unit B.

5. Sew Unit A to Unit B so that the small feature triangles look like a split triangle, as per the block diagram.

6. Refer to the block diagram to sew two 1½" × 6½" background rectangles (C), two 1½" × 6½" feature fabric rectangles (X) and one 2½" × 6½" background rectangle (I) together. Press. Sew a 6½" × 6½" background square (S) to the top. Press.

7. Sew the two halves together.

Block 2

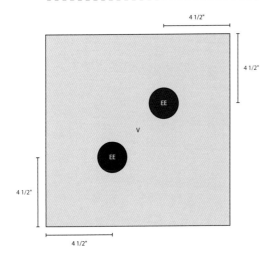

1. Refer to page 86 to create two freezer paper templates circles with finished diameters of 2".

2. Cut out the circle templates. Press the shiny side of one template to the wrong side of one 3" × 3" feature fabric squares (EE). Repeat with the second template and square.

3. Follow the instructions on page 86 for gathering and pressing to create the appliqué circle.

4. Measure 4½" up and 4½ " across from the bottom left corner and from the top right corner of a 12½" × 12½" background square (V) and make a small marking. Find the centers of the circles (see Quilter to Quilter on page 84) and pin on the background over the marks.

5. Appliqué the circles to the background with coordinating thread and preferred stitch. Press.

Block 3

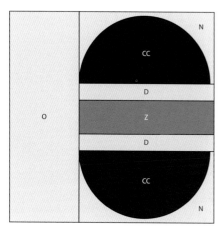

1. Refer to page 86 to create two freezer paper templates for inset half circle blocks with a finished diameter of 8".

2. Cut out the half circles. Press the shiny side of the templates to the wrong sides of two 4½" × 8½" feature fabric rectangles (CC). Press the shiny side of the background templates to the wrong sides of two 4½" × 8½" background rectangles (N).

3. Refer to the instructions on page 90 for sewing inset curves. Fold and mark registration points on the curves; pin and sew one half circle and one background together. Press. Repeat with the remaining pieces. Trim to 4½" × 8½". Press. Repeat.

4. Add a 1½" × 8½" background rectangle (D) to the bottom of each half circle. Press. Join the two half circle sections together with a 2½" × 8½" feature fabric rectangle (Z) as shown in the block diagram. Press.

5. Sew a 4½" × 12½" background rectangle (O) to the left side. Press.

Block 4

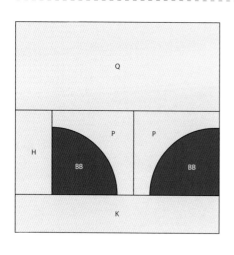

1. Refer to page 90 to create two freezer paper templates for the inset quarter circle blocks with a finished radius of 4".

2. Cut out the quarter circles. Press the shiny side of each quarter circle template to the wrong side of a 4½" × 4½" feature fabric square (BB). Press the shiny side of each background template to the wrong side of a 5½" × 5½" background square (P).

3. Refer to the instructions on page 90 for sewing inset curves. Fold and mark registration points on the curves; pin and sew one quarter circle to one background. Press. Repeat with the remaining pieces. Trim to 5½" × 5½".

4. Sew the two quarter circle blocks together in mirror image; press. Add a 2½" × 5½" background rectangle (H) to the left side; press.

5. Sew the 5 ½" × 12½" rectangle (Q) to the top and a 2½" × 12½" rectangle (K) to the bottom. Press.

Block 5

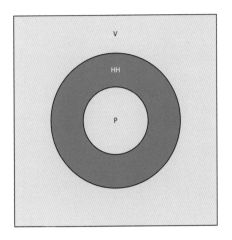

1. Refer to page 86 to create freezer paper templates for a reverse circle. Cut two 12½" × 12½" squares. Draw an 8" circle in the center of one square and a 4" circle in the center of the second square. Cut out the circles.

2. Apply the template with the 8" circle cutout to the wrong side of one 12½" × 12½" background square (V). Leaving a ½" seam allowance, cut the circle out of the fabric and prepare the piece to apply a reverse circle. See page 89 for detailed instructions.

3. Glue and sew a 9" × 9" feature fabric square (HH) to the wrong side of the background square. Press. Trim excess feature fabric.

4. Apply the template with the 4" circle cut out of it to the wrong side of the block from Step 3. Cut out the smaller circle and prep the piece to apply a reverse circle. This time the fringe will be cut from the feature fabric.

5. Glue and sew a 5½" × 5½" background square (P) to the circle opening. Press and trim excess fabric.

Block 6

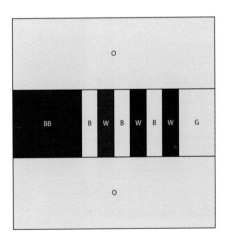

1. Refer to the diagram to lay out and sew the following pieces: three 1½" × 4½" background rectangles (B), one 2½" × 4½" background rectangle (G), three 1½" × 4½" feature fabric rectangles (W), and one 4½" × 4½" feature fabric square (BB). Press.

2. Add a 4½" × 12½" background rectangle (O) to the top and bottom. Press.

Block 7

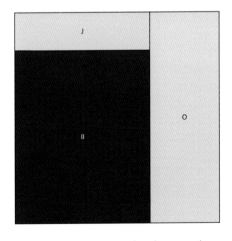

1. Sew a 2½" × 8½" background rectangle (J) to the top of the 8½" × 10½" feature fabric rectangle (II). Press.

2. Add a 4½" × 12½" background rectangle (O) to the right side. Press.

Block 8

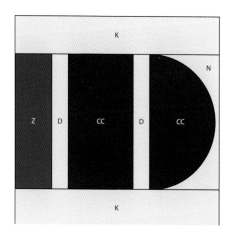

1. Refer to page 86 to create a freezer paper template for the inset half circle block with a finished diameter of 8".

2. Cut out the half circle. Press the shiny side of the half circle template to the wrong side of a 4½" × 8½" feature fabric rectangle (CC). Press the background template to the wrong side of a 4½" × 8½" background rectangle (N).

3. Refer to the instructions on page 90 for sewing inset curves.

Fold and mark registration points on the curves; pin and sew together. Press. Trim to 4½" × 8½".

4. Sew the following strip set: 1½" × 8½" background rectangle (D), 4½" × 8½" feature fabric rectangle (CC), 1½" × 8½" background rectangle (D), and 2½" × 8½" feature fabric rectangle (Z). Sew the strip set to the left of the half circle.

5. Add a 2½" × 12½" background strip (K) to the top and bottom. Press.

Block 9

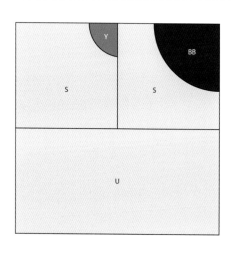

1. Refer to page 86 to create two freezer paper templates for the inset quarter circle blocks, one with a finished radius of 4" and the other 2".

2. Cut out the quarter circles. Press the shiny side of the small quarter circle template to the wrong side of a 2½"x 2½" feature fabric square (Y) and the large quarter circle to a 4½" × 4½" feature fabric square (BB). Press the shiny side of each background template to the wrong side of two 6½" × 6½" background squares (S).

3. Refer to the instructions on page 90 for sewing inset curves. Fold and mark registration points on the curves; pin and sew one quarter circle and one background together. Press. Repeat with the remaining pieces. Trim to 6½" × 6½".

4. Sew the two quarter circle blocks together as shown in the block diagram. Sew a 6½" × 12½" background rectangle (U) to the bottom. Press.

Block 10

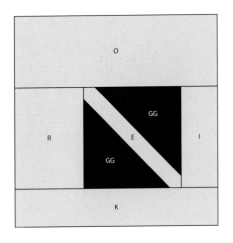

1. Cut one 7" × 7" feature square (GG) in half on the diagonal to create two triangles.

2. Sew one 1½" × 1 ½"background strip (E) along the diagonal edge of one triangle. Line up the second triangle to keep the points when trimming and sew to the background strip. Press. Trim to 6½"x 6½".

3. Sew a 2½" × 6½" background rectangle (I) to the right side of the block from Step 2 and the 4½" × 6½" background rectangle (R) to the left. Press. Add a 2½" × 12½" background rectangle (K) to the bottom and a 4½" × 12½" background rectangle (O) to the top. Press.

Block 11

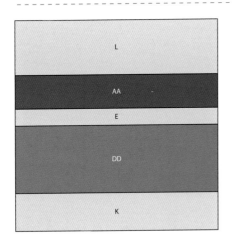

1. Refer to the diagram and sew together the strips from top to bottom in this order: 3½" × 12½" background rectangle (L), 2½" × 12½" feature fabric rectangle (AA), 1½" × 12½" background rectangle (E), 4½" × 12½" feature fabric rectangle (DD), and 2½" × 12½" background rectangle (K). Press.

Block 12

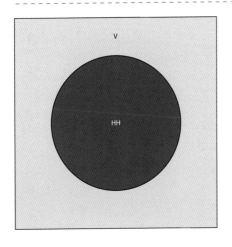

1. Refer to page 86 to create a freezer paper template for a circle with a finished diameter of 8".

2. Cut out the circle template. Press the shiny side of the template to the wrong side of a 9" × 9" feature fabric square (HH).

3. Follow the instructions on page 86 for gathering and pressing to create the appliqué circle.

4. Center the circle on a 12½"x 12½" background square (V). Pin and appliqué using coordinating thread and your preferred stitch. Press.

Block 13

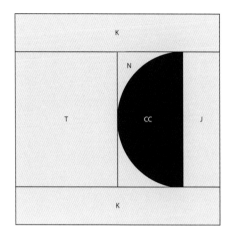

1. Refer to page 86 to create the freezer paper template for the inset half circle block with a finished diameter of 8".

2. Cut out the half circle. Press the shiny side of the half circle template to the wrong side of a 4½" × 8½" feature fabric rectangle (CC). Press the background template to the wrong side of a 4½" × 8½" background rectangle (N). Add a ¼" seam allowance when cutting.

3. Refer to the instructions on page 90 for sewing inset curves. Fold and mark registration points on the curves; pin and sew together. Press.

4. Add a 2½" × 8 ½" background rectangle (J) to the right side of the half circle and a 6½" × 8½" background rectangle (T) to the left. Press. Sew a 2½" × 12½" rectangle (K) to the top and bottom. Press.

Block 14

1. Refer to diagram to lay out and sew together these pieces: two 2½" × 12 ½" background rectangles (K), two 2½" × 12½" feature fabric rectangles (AA), and one 4½" × 12½" feature fabric rectangle (DD). Press.

Block 15

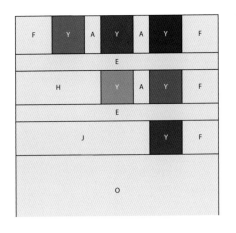

1. Assemble the top row in this order: 2½" × 2½" background square (F), 2½" × 2½" feature fabric square (Y), 1½" × 2½" background rectangle (A), 2½" × 2½" feature fabric square (Y), 1½" × 2½" background rectangle (A), 2½"x 2½" feature fabric square (Y), and 2½" × 2½" background square (F). Press. Add a 1½" × 12½" background strip (E) to the bottom. Press.

2. Sew together the middle row in this order: 2½" × 5½" background rectangle (H), 2½" × 2½" feature fabric square (Y), 1½"x 2½" background rectangle (A), 2½" × 2½" feature fabric square (Y), and 2½" × 2½" background square (F). Press. Add a 1½" × 12½" background strip (E) to the bottom. Press.

3. Sew together the bottom row in this order: 2½"x 8½" background rectangle (J), 2½" × 2½" feature fabric square (Y), and 2½" × 2½" background square (F). Press. Add a 4½" × 12½" background rectangle (O) to the bottom. Press.

4. Refer to the diagram and assemble the block. Press.

Block 16

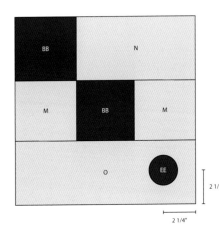

1. Refer to page 86 to create the freezer paper template for a circle with a finished diameter of 2".

2. Cut out the circle template. Press the shiny side of the template to the wrong side of a 3" × 3" feature fabric square (EE).

3. Follow the instructions on page 87 for gathering and pressing to create the appliqué circle.

4. Mark a point 2¼" across and 2¼" up from the bottom right corner of a 4½" × 12½" background rectangle (O). Center the circle appliqué on this point. Pin and appliqué using coordinating thread and your favorite stitch. Press.

5. Sew a 4½" × 4½" feature square (BB) to a 4½" × 8½" background rectangle (N).

6. Sew a 4½" × 4½" background square (M) to each side of a 4½" × 4½" feature fabric square (BB).

7. Refer to the diagram and sew the rows together to complete the block. Press.

ASSEMBLING THE QUILT TOP

1. Lay out the quilt blocks in numerical order. There are four blocks in each row and a total of four rows. Sew the blocks together in rows, then sew the rows together. Press.

2. Cut one strip in half and attach to two 12½" x width of fabric strips. Trim each to 48½". Attach two 12½" x width of fabric strips together and trim to 72½". Repeat for remaining two strips.

3. Pin and sew one short border to the right and left sides of the quilt top center. Press. Pin and sew the long strips to the top and bottom. Press.

FINISHING THE QUILT

1. Piece the backing to 80" × 80". Layer backing, batting, and quilt top; baste as desired.

2. Quilt with an all-over design and thread that works with both the graphic elements and background to add texture to the entire quilt, or quilt the background and graphic elements separately.

3. Cut eight 2½" wide binding strips and join with diagonal seams. Fold the strip in half, wrong sides together, and press. Bind the quilt with a ¼" seam allowance.

PAPER PIECING
A PRACTICE WORKSHOP

TEACHER:
Penny Layman

Goal of Class: Paper piecing is the easiest way to ensure the most accurate points possible. In my workshop, we will go over the basics so you can have fun making a single block to use in smaller projects (a pillow, mug rug, bag panel, or mini-quilt) or create intricate, more graphic blocks that can be set into a grid for larger quilts. Either way, by adding these techniques to your toolbox, you will never look at your smallest scrap in the same way again.

Introducing Paper Piecing

Cherry Jam Jar.

MODERN QUILT MAKING AND PAPER PIECING

I consider myself a vintage modern quilter, utilizing vintage and retro aspects in my designs and/or fabrics. Also, I often use paper piecing techniques for my quilts and quilty projects to create bold geometrics and simple to complex object designs that result in edgy (or sweet), modern blocks and quilts.

FOUNDATION SUBSTRATES

Fabric and paper are the most common substrate materials for foundation piecing. If you piece onto a fabric layer, the base layer of fabric is a part of the finished piece. If you piece onto paper, the paper is removed once the block is completed.

There are several foundation piecing papers available. Some are thin, making the removal process easy. Some papers are made of vellum, which makes fussy cutting easier since you can see through the vellum to cut the precise area of fabric you desire.

QUILTER TO QUILTER

I recommend that beginners use the paper specifically designed for paper piecing, but it's expensive. Switch to 20 lb. standard copy/printer paper as soon as you are comfortable. It's thin, inexpensive, and easy to find.

READING YOUR PATTERN

As you begin to foundation piece, it is important to know how to read a pattern. Most will be color coded **(Fig. 1)**, but if not **(Fig. 2)**, color in or otherwise mark each area with the color of fabric. This way, you won't get confused and sew the wrong fabric to a section.

Sections are indicated by letters. If you have a pattern with no letters **(Fig. 3)**, the pattern is all one section and can be sewn as one piece. The numbers indicate the order of sewing. If your pattern has letters **(Fig. 4)**, the pattern must be cut into sections, the sections pieced in number order, then the sections sewn together.

The cutting lines on a pattern are indicated by bolder lines and/or a different colored line, such as the blue line in **Figure 4.** The thinner black lines are sewing lines.

When a pattern has more than one section, tick marks on the cutting lines are helpful in positioning the sections as you sew (red lines in **Fig. 4**). If your pattern does not have tick marks, you can add your own before cutting your pattern pieces apart.

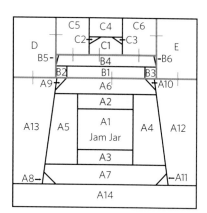

Figure 1

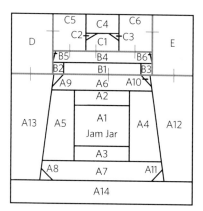

Figure 2

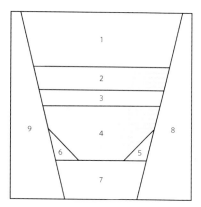

Figure 3

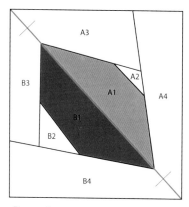

Figure 4

ENGLISH PAPER PIECING

Not to be confused with English paper piecing, which is sewn by hand, this type of paper piecing is sewn by machine. The block design is printed on paper and then the fabrics are sewn onto the unprinted side of the paper. Once the block is completed, the paper is removed and you are left with your fabric block.

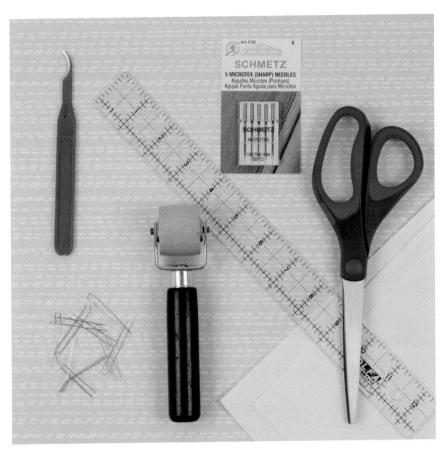

Paper piecing supplies.

NECESSARY SUPPLIES

Whether you're a woodworker creating beautiful furniture, or a paper piecer creating amazing quilts, there are specific tools every artist needs to be efficient and effective with her or his chosen craft.

Printed Pattern

First, you will need your printed pattern. For this workshop, you will photocopy the pages in this book; when you print patterns from your computer, make sure that you always check the box that reads "actual size" in the printer set-up screen. Once you print the pattern, double check the printed block size so you don't end up with an inaccurately scaled pattern.

Your pattern is the mirror image of what your block will look like, so your pattern is the reverse of your finished block. Sometimes it takes a little while for this concept to sink in, but it will get better the more you paper piece, I promise.

Needle and Presser Foot

When it comes to your sewing machine, use a microtex 80 needle (also called a sharp needle). It has a slim point and is perfect for ensuring accuracy in your piecing (shown).

I don't pay attention to the guide as I'm piecing each section (that is what the pattern is for!), but I do recommend using a ¼" presser foot with a guide as you sew sections together to ensure accurate seams.

Seam Roller

One of my favorite must-have tools for paper piecing is a seam roller (shown). It presses evenly, without distorting the fabric, and makes the assembly process go so much more quickly. Don't confuse a fabric seam roller with a wallpaper seam roller. Wallpaper seam rollers are flat and about 3" wide. The sharper, flat edges can catch your fabric and mar it as you roll. A fabric seam roller is 1" wide and has a curved surface and edge.

Seam Ripper/Stitch Picker

As wrong as this may sound, I'm going to say it anyway. Another favorite tool is my seam ripper, also called a stitch picker. A sharp and thin point is a must. Yes, seam rippers get dull just like your rotary cutter blades, but over a longer period of time. I use the Pro Seam-Ripper (shown) from leevalley.com. I like how sharp it is; when it starts to dull, I can put a new a new blade on it. I would not, however, recommend this type for quilters who have small children in the house. Instead, I would choose a seam ripper that has a less exposed blade. Seam picking happens often when paper piecing, and having a seam ripper with a sharp blade makes this tedious task go more quickly.

Craft Scissors

Most quilters use their sewing scissors exclusively for cutting fabric. I recommend having a second pair of craft scissors (shown) on hand for cutting your paper pattern.

Fabric Glue Stick

Rather than using pins to hold your fabric against the paper pattern back (pins can often pull and distort the fabric), I recommend using a fabric glue stick. My favorite is the Karisma Fabric Glue Stick, which doesn't leave a residue. Karisma can be difficult to find, so a good alternative is the water-soluable stick from Fons & Porter which is easier to find in the US, and has refills like the Karisma glue stick.

I also recommend using a glue stick when the first piece of fabric in a section is large. Gluing the fabric to the paper stabalizes larger fabric pieces as you attach the remaining sections. The glue stick creates just enough of a bond between the fabric and the paper.

Freezer Paper and Tracing Paper

Two more tools that are handy on occasion are freezer paper and Saral tracing paper. You can find freezer paper in rolls at the grocery store or in sheets from specialty quilting shops. I prefer to use the sheets because they are pre-cut to 8½ × 11" so they go through the printer easily (shown). You will use freezer paper when you are fussy cutting an area or single piece section, for appliqué, and for special Y seams. You will use the Saral tracing paper to trace an embroidery design onto the block after it's been pieced.

Other Necessities

Other tools that are a must are a 1" × 12" acrylic ruler with a ¼" seam mark (shown), a small- to medium-size rotary cutter, a self-healing rotary mat, and fork pins (shown). Fork pins are a helpful tool to keep your seams matched up as you sew.

PAPER PIECING STEP-BY-STEP

Let's start by sewing a simple, one section pattern (see page 190 for bowl template). I've used vellum so that you can more easily see the printed image through the backside of the pattern. Once you have mastered the basics, we will move on to the leaf block (see page 190 for template) so that you can practice joining sections using tick marks.

Single Sectioned Bowl Block

1. Print then cut out the block pattern close to outside lines.

My preference is to cut out the pattern close to the outside block lines (and directly down the middle of the cutting lines if the pattern has sections) instead of including a ¼" seam allowance around the entire paper pattern and its sections. This way, as you sew the sections together, you won't be sewing paper into the seams, which will make removal of the paper at the end a lot easier.

QUILTER TO QUILTER

When a sewing line begins and/or ends on the outside edge of the block, make sure to start sewing the fabric together at least ¼" before and/or ¼" after the paper pattern.

2. Cut fabrics for each area.

Pre-cutting the fabrics for each area will keep you moving forward and reduce confusion as you sew. Keep in mind that not only does the fabric need to cover the area, it needs to overlap the area by at least ¼". Also, make sure the fabric for all areas that are part of the outside edges of the block (Areas 1, 7, 8, and 9 are the outside areas in this pattern) extend at least ¼" past the edge of the paper pattern. This will be your block seam allowance when you are done. Once the pieces are cut, stack them with the Area 1 piece on the top and the Area 9 piece on the bottom. This will allow you to pull the top piece off and quickly sew it to the next area instead of having to stop and cut the next piece of fabric.

3. Position the first piece of fabric and lightly glue into place **(Fig. 5)**.

The first fabric you place will always be wrong side toward the paper. As you place your fabric, you want to make sure it extends at least ¼" past all edges of the area you are using it in.

QUILTER TO QUILTER

Before doing any cutting, you should double and triple check to make sure you are cutting the fabric on the correct side of the seam. As you cut, your fabrics should still be right sides together and not flipped open.

4. Position the second piece of fabric.

The second piece of fabric will always be right side to the paper or right sides together with the first fabric **(Fig. 6)**. The raw edge that will become your ¼" seam allowance is always positioned to be partially lying in the area you will be covering. This step seems counterintuitive to most people, so just have faith!

5. Sew the first and second fabrics together **(Fig. 7)**.

With the paper side facing up, sew the first and second fabrics together on the sewing line between Areas 1 and 2. Your stitch length should be adjusted

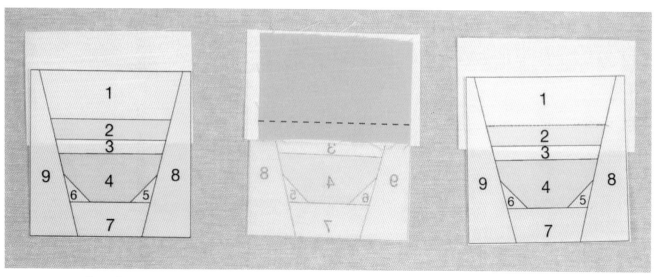

Figure 5   Figure 6   Figure 7

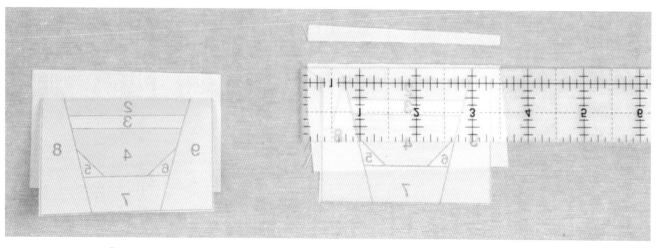

Figure 8   Figure 9

to 1.6-1.8 before you sew. If the sewing line begins or ends within the block, go ahead and backstitch wherever that occurs. For this pattern, you will be backstitching at the beginning and end of sewing when adding fabrics 2, 3, 4, 5, 6, and 7 since all these sewing lines begin and end within the block.

6. Trim the seam.

Fold the paper back along the seam you just sewed **(Fig. 8)**. Place your block on your cutting mat. Use your ruler and rotary cutter to trim the seam by placing the ¼" line along the seam line and trim the fabric with a rotary cutter **(Fig. 9)**.

7. Press the seam line flat.

Turn your block back over to the fabric side and flip open the fabric you just sewed onto the block that covers the second area. Finger-press the seam area open and follow behind with the seam roller

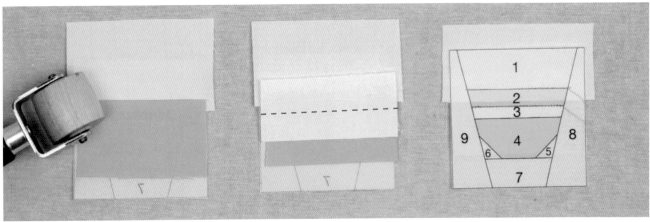

Figure 10   Figure 11   Figure 12

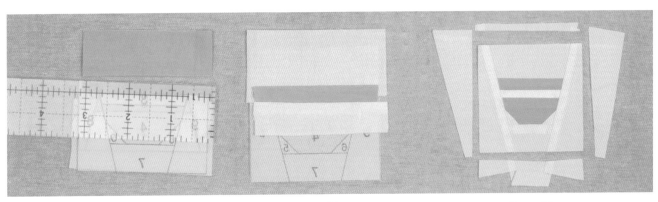

Figure 13   Figure 14   Figure 15

to press the seam line flat **(Fig. 10)**. If your seam isn't completely opened, you will end up with a little pocket in the seam as well as puckering, and your seams won't match up correctly.

8. Position the third piece of fabric.

The third fabric is a bit trickier to position. To make it easier, I will often crease the second fabric corresponding to the sewing line between Areas 2 and 3 and then place the edge of the third fabric at least ¼" over this line **(Fig. 11)**.

9. Sew the second and third fabrics together.

Sew the next two fabrics together on the sewing line between Areas 2 and 3, following the same instructions in Step 5 **(Fig. 12)**.

10. Place your block on your cutting mat. Use your ruler and rotary cutter to trim the seam **(Fig. 13)**.

Again, make sure you are trimming the correct side of the seam.

11. Press the seam line flat with a seam roller **(Fig. 14)**.

12. Repeat Steps 8 through 11, positioning, sewing, trimming and rolling, until each area of the block is pieced. Press block with starch.

14. Trim the fabric to ¼" past the paper pattern (or section) edges. **(Fig. 15)**.

15. Remove paper from the block in reverse order from the sewing order by folding the paper back over the seam line. Creasing the fold with your finger, and pulling the paper off as if you are pulling a check out of your checkbook.

Two Sectioned Leaf Block

Piecing a block that has more than one section adds just a couple of steps to the process. The biggest difference is that in addition to cutting around the paper pattern edges, you will also cut on any cutting lines in the pattern which are often indicated with a different colored line. Print out pattern from 190 then you follow Steps 2 through 14 for each section. These sections will in turn need to be sewn together in the end after they are each pieced.

The last step is to sew the sections together. To do this, lay the sections right sides together and put pins straight through the fabric on the front section, right where the tick mark on that section comes to the edge of the paper pattern.

Shift the sections around slightly until the pins are basically perpendicular to the blocks. This will be the indicator that the sections are aligned. Hold the sections together this way and pin the sections together like normal and remove the perpendicular pins. Sew the sections together with a ¼" seam, press the seam open, and remove the paper from the back.

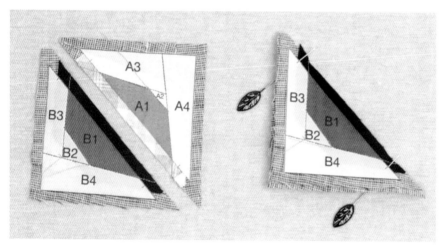

Two pieced section.

Align pins in both edges of the sections at tick marks.

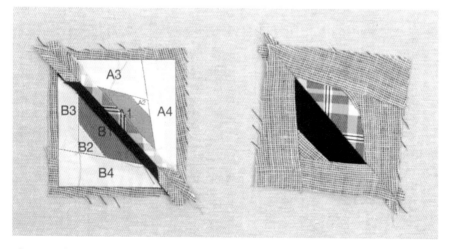

Sew together with ¼" seem allowance.

Press and remove paper from back.

TROUBLESHOOTING GUIDE

Classroom advice from Penny.

PRINTING PATTERNS

If you prefer your finished block to be facing the same dierction as your original paper pattern, you can reverse the paper pattern by scanning the pattern into your computer and using photo software to reverse the image. You can then print the new reversed pattern and piece it.

CUTTING FABRICS

When paper piecing, it can appear that only a tiny piece of fabric is needed for an area. It can be frustrating to find out after you've sewn the fabric into place and flipped the fabric open, that the piece is just shy of covering the area you needed or isn't big enough to allow for a seam allowance. Because of this, always use a piece of fabric that is larger than what you think you will need for each area.

PRESSING SEAMS

When you press a seam open, the fabrics on either side of the seam will have a flat appearance from the front. Also, when you run your hand over the front of the work, it will have a smoother feel.

When you press a seam to the side, the direction that the seam is pressed toward will stand out a bit more, and the side you press the seam away from will recede. You will also be able to feel this "stair step" effect when you run your hand over the front of the work.

Since foundation piecing patterns have the directions of the seams already laid out according to how each section is numbered (the seam will always be pressed to the side of the larger number as you add fabric), the only time you will have to consider how to press a seam is if the pattern has more than one section.

CHOOSING FABRICS

As you choose fabrics, consider how busy the fabrics are together. Lay your fabric choices next to one another and if your brain seizes, you might want to tone it down a bit by putting some solids or small prints in your selection.

Evaluate the size of print on the fabric compared to the size of the area you are filling. If the area is tiny but the print is large, you should reconsider the print you've chosen.

  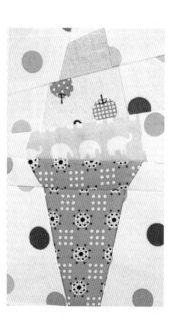

With this block, there is no place for your eye to rest. There are too many large prints going too many directions, and most of the prints have a cream color to them that blends with the background print too much.

This block still has too many different prints. Another thing that sticks out to me is that the color of the bottom layer of ice cream is too much like the background.

The main thing I would change with this block would be to choose a smaller print for the bottom two layers of ice cream.

ADDING EMBELLISHMENTS

You've heard it said before, "It's all in the details." With paper piecing, those small details make a big difference. Not only with the fabrics you choose, from the background print to the fussy cut areas, but also in the final touches you might add after a block is pieced. The embellishments that sing to me are stamping, hand embroidery, and appliqué.

Walk This Way mug rug.

Embroidery

Out of all the embellishing I have done, embroidery is my favorite. It is super easy to transfer your embroidery pattern to your block using Saral tracing paper and an embossing (tracing) tool. Add your embroidery after the block is completely pieced, but before binding or piecing into a larger project. I used this technique for the hand mixer project block.

Stamping

If you are going to stamp a portion of a block, here are some things to consider.

1. Use a permanent fabric ink.

I've also been experimenting with pigment ink pads. Pigment ink pads have a very saturated color and can readily be found in stamping supply stores. However, because of the way pigment inks work, I would not use them on any project that will be washed, only on wall hangings.

2. Stamp your image/words on the fabric before it is pieced into the block, don't wait until you've pieced your block to stamp on it in case you make a mistake.

3. Use your printer to "stamp" words. If your project requires larger or different stamps than you have on hand, use your printer to print on your fabric. The steps are time consuming, but well worth it.

Pretreat your fabric with Bubble Jet Set™ and allow the fabric to dry. Iron onto an 8½ x 11 piece of freezer paper and trim excess fabric. Print the image on the fabric using your printer and set the ink by ironing. Remove the paper, treat with the Bubble Jet Set™ rinse and allow to dry.

Appliqué

I like to add appliqué when I want the image to stand out a bit, or if the block design will become too cumbersome if it is pieced. Appliqué can be added after your block is pieced, by following these steps.

1. Print the appliqué design onto freezer paper.

2. Cut out the design.

3. Iron the shiny side of the freezer paper to the back side of the fabric.

Juice Bar quilt.

4. Trim the fabric to ⅛" to ¼" past the paper.

5. Press the fabric around the edges of the paper using a good dose of starch and an iron.

6. Remove the freezer paper from the fabric back and turn under the edges using your favorite technique.

7. Glue the appliqué to the area you desire with a small bead of water-soluble fabric glue to hold the appliqué in place.

8. Use an invisible stitch to stitch the appliqué down.

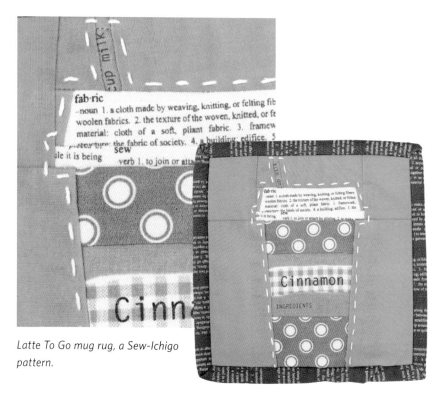

Latte To Go mug rug, a Sew-Ichigo pattern.

crazy glasses

fedora

shopping bag

sunny dress

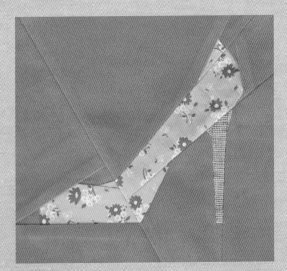

stiletto

Paper Piecing Projects

For each block below, print out the appropriate pattern (pages 180-190) to size and cut as close to the outside edges as possible. When all of the sections are cut, complete all sections, working in the numbered order and making sure to leave at least ¼″ of fabric past all edges of each section. Trim a ¼″ seam allowance past the paper pattern edges of each section as show on the Leaf block on page 115.

FEDORA

5" × 6"

Fabrics

10" square for background
8" square for hat
2" × 6" rectangle for band

Instructions

1. Cut the block into two sections (A and B) on the blue lines.
2. Join A to B. Press seam open.
3. Press block with starch. Trim to 5½" × 6½".

Based on original artwork by Robert Blackard for Rob and Bob Studio.

CRAZY GLASSES

7¾" × 7¾"

Fabrics

Fat eighth for background
10" square for glasses

Instructions

1. Cut the block into eight sections (A through H) on the blue lines.
2. Join A to B. Press seam open.
3. Join C to AB. Press seam open.
4. Join G to H. Press seam toward H.

5. Join E to F. Press seam toward F.
6. Join GH to D. Press seam open.
7. Join EF to DGH. Press seam open.
8. Join ABC to DEFGH. Press seam open.
9. Press block with starch. Trim to 8¼" × 8¼".

SUNNY DRESS

5" × 10"

Fabrics

Fat eighth for background
7" square for orange strips and straps
7" square for yellow strips
3" square for hanger

Instructions

1. Cut the block into twelve sections (A through L) on the blue lines.
2. Join A to B. Press seam open.
3. Join C to D. Press seam open.
4. Join AB to CD. Press seam open.
5. Join E and F to ABCD. Press seams open.
6. Join G and H to ABCDEF. Press seams toward G and H.

7. Join I to J. Press seam open.
8. Join K and L to IJ. Press seams toward K and L.
9. Join ABCDEFGH to IJKL. Press seam open.
10. Press block with starch. Trim to 5½" × 10½".

STILETTO

6½" × 7½"

Fabrics

Fat quarter for background,
10" square for shoe
5" square for heel

Instructions

1. Cut the block into six sections (A through F) on the blue lines.
2. Join A to B. Press seam open.
3. Join C, D, and E. Press seams open.
4. Join AB to CDE. Press seam toward AB.
5. Join F to ABCDE. Press seam open.
6. Press block with starch. Trim to 7" × 8".

SHOPPING BAG

8" × 8"

Fabrics

Fat eighth for background
6" square for handle
8" square for main bag
4" × 8" rectangle for bag bottom.

Instructions

1. Cut the block into four sections (A through D) on the blue lines.
2. Join A, B, and C. Press seams open.
3. Join D to ABC. Press seam open.
4. Press block with starch. Trim to 8½" × 8½".

CANOLA

6" × 6"

Fabrics

Fat eighth for background
4" × 8" blue rectangle
9" yellow square
3" orange square

Instructions

1. Cut the block into two sections (A and B) on the blue lines.
2. Join A to B. Press seam open.
3. Press block with starch. Trim to 6½" × 6½".

PROPELLER

8" × 8"

Fabrics

Fat quarter for background
6" square for small blue accent
5" square for each larger accent

Instructions

1. Cut the block into two sections (A and B) on the blue lines.
2. Join A to B. Press seam open.
3. Press block with starch. Trim to 8½" × 8½".

HAND MIXER

8" × 9"

Fabrics/Notions

Fat quarter for background
6" square for plug and beaters
4" square for beater to mixer body area
7" square for mixer body
3" square for buttons
embroidery thread for cord

Instructions

1. Cut the block into twelve sections (A through L) on the blue lines.
2. Join B to C. Press seam open.
3. Join A to BC. Press seam open.
4. Join D, E, F, G, H, I together. Press seams open.
5. Join DEFGHI to K. Press seams open.
6. Join J and L to DEFGHIK. Press seam open.
7. Join ABC to DEFGHIJKL. Press seam open.
8. Join M to ABCDEFGHIJKL. Press seams open.
9. Press block with starch. Trim to 8¼" × 9¼".
10. Trace cord from template on page 184 with tracing paper and embroider with a backstitch.

BEACH BALL

8" × 8"

Fabrics

Fat eighth for background
9" square for center accent
5" square for each smaller accent

Instructions

1. Cut the block into three sections (A through C) on the blue lines.
2. Join A, B, and C. Press seams open.
3. Press block with starch. Trim to 8½" × 8½".

SNOW CONES

6½" × 10"

Fabrics

Fat quarter for background
10" square for paper containers
5" square for each snow cone top

Instructions

1. Cut the block into six sections (A through F) on the blue lines.
2. Join A, B, and C. Press seams open.
3. Join D, E, and F. Press seam open.
4. Join ABC to DEF. Press seam open.
5. Press block with starch. Trim to 7" × 10½".

propeller

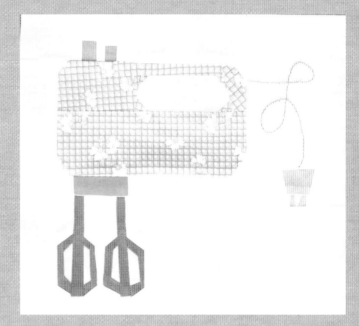

hand mixer

canola

beach ball

snow cones

LARGE-SCALE PIECING

A PRACTICE WORKSHOP

Goal of Class: In this workshop, you will learn the benefits of large-scale piecing and constructing oversize blocks. While the approach may look straightforward enough, working with large pieces of fabric presents its own set of challenges... and rewards. We'll go over some composition decisions brought up by this style of piecing, and explore how to work with large areas of negative space.

TEACHER: Heather Jones

Large-Scale Piecing in Modern Quilts

WHAT IS LARGE-SCALE PIECING?

I define large-scale piecing in block-based quilting as using anything larger than 12" finished blocks. Large-scale piecing can consist of quilt blocks of any type of traditional pattern with an increase in size, or it can be constructed through strip piecing or working with large areas of negative space, which I will talk more about below.

Typically, quilts that are constructed through large-scale piecing have fewer pieces that make up their overall design. These quilts, by their very nature, are more simplified due to this decreased number of pattern pieces. To put this in perspective, think of a twin-size quilt that is made up of 12" blocks; it would have a minimum of 48 of those blocks, without sashing. Now, say those blocks are something simple, like a nine-patch pattern; that twin-size quilt would be made up of approximately 432 pieces. The same twin-size quilt made with large-scale piecing, say using 20" square blocks, would consist of only 12 blocks and 108 pieces.

MODERN ART

Large-scale piecing is a hallmark of modern quilt making. This approach has roots in works of fine art from the twentieth century—particularly influenced by the paintings of Mark Rothko, Elsworth Kelly, Helen Frankenthaler, and Josef Albers—which show that increasing the scale, or size, of a design of any type can add more drama to the overall composition.

DESIGNING CONSIDERATIONS

The reduction in the number of pattern pieces simplifies the quilt pattern, regardless of the way the quilt is constructed and no matter what the pattern. One of my favorite ways to work is to simplify a traditional quilt pattern by focusing on just one element of the overall design and increase its scale. I will often block and increase the size so that it makes up the majority of the quilt top itself.

Ebb and Flow

This play on scale was my approach with Ebb and Flow, the project I designed for this workshop, which is a large-scale version of a traditional churn dash block. Typically, this block would be made at a much smaller scale (such as 12" finished), and the finished quilt would consist of many of the same size blocks, all pieced together to form a quilt top, with or without sashing.

My Ohio Supernova quilt (left) is an example of large-scale piecing where one block makes up the majority of the design of the quilt top. In my You + Me quilt (right), I've used four large-scale blocks with sashing in the design.

That is the case with this churn dash quilt that was made by my great-great aunt Ollie Logsdon. She was an avid quilter, and this quilt was probably made in the 1960s or 1970s. Her quilt measures 64" × 81" and is made up of eighty 8" blocks.

In my version, I have increased the scale of the churn dash block so that the quilt top consists of just one block. While a traditional churn dash quilt project could consist of blocks ranging in size anywhere from 3" to 12", the "block" in my project measures a whopping 68".

SIMPLIFY

It is fairly easy to understand the concept that increasing the scale simplifies a pattern, but what makes these traditional blocks look so modern is that playing with scale to this degree is also reductive. This means that the overall design is reduced to its most important features. There is no room for excessive design elements; only large areas of clean lines and color are left when the scale is increased so greatly, which furthers the quilt's modern aesthetic. Working on this scale also produces more dramatic designs.

Another one of my favorite examples of this type of large-scale piecing is my Ohio Supernova quilt. The design consists of a

Anni's simple sophistication derives from the four large-scale monochromatic quilt blocks.

Me quilt. It features only four 28" square blocks that are are pieced together to create the top with minimal sashing.

Playing With Scale

The quilt that I titled Gelassenheit could be considered a hybrid of two types of large-scale patchwork construction. It is composed of a classic block design that has been dramatically increased in size, plus oversize blocks that have been pieced out of strips of fabric. A large-scale Dresden plate block has been appliquéd onto a background of four strip-pieced large-scale blocks. The Dresden plate block measures 19½" tip to tip, and the quilt itself is 54" square.

CREATING NEGATIVE SPACE

The final type of large-scale piecing technique that I use often is to combine a small number of large-scale blocks with a lot of negative space. This is a great way to draw focus to the individual blocks in a quilt.

My linen mini-quilt is a good example of incorporating large amounts of negative space. Negative space is the space around and between the quilt block or blocks (often referred to in patterns as the "background") that are often the focal point of the overall com-

classic Ohio star block that has been increased drastically to make up the vast majority of the quilt's design. The finished quilt is 73½" × 73½".

OVERSIZE BLOCKS

Another type of large-scale piecing is a design in which a series of oversize quilt blocks are constructed and sewn together to make a quilt top. This is the case with my You + Me quilt, which is made up of four large quilt blocks.

These blocks are constructed using a series of long strips of fabric to complete a pieced design that looks like stripes, which are then subcut into squares. Four of those squares are sewn together with wide sashing and a keystone block to create one large quilt block, each measuring 28". The four quilt blocks are then finished with a thin band of sashing and a wide border to complete the overall design.

My Anni quilt is another example of using large-scale quilt blocks. This quilt is simpler in both design and construction than my You +

position. However, when used in conjunction with large-scale piecing, the negative space actually often becomes a focal point itself.

My linen mini-quilt features a single improvised log cabin block. The block itself is relatively busy; you can imagine that the overall composition of the quilt would be much more overwhelming if I had used a large number of these blocks without any negative space. This combination of large areas of negative space and large-scale piecing brings sophistication and a clean line to the design.

If you are looking to incorporate blocks from the Improvisational Patchwork workshop on page 52, consider creating a composition that surrounds a few blocks with lots of negative space like this— perhaps even combining it with an alternate setting style from the Alternate Grid workshop on page 62.

Due to the increase in scale of the pieced blocks in a quilt composition, the role of the negative space in modern quilt making becomes a more important design element.

My great-aunt Ollie's churn dash quilt. Each of these blocks measures approximately 8", which is a traditional scale for this design.

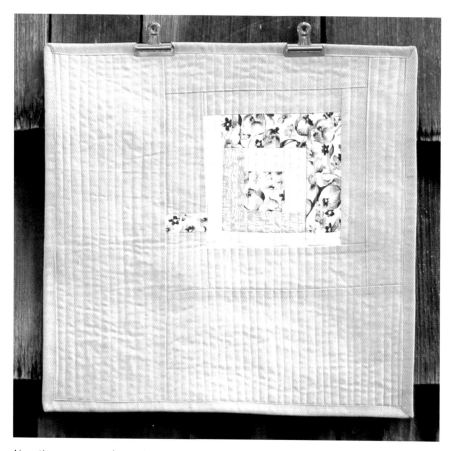

Negative space can play an important role in large-scale piecing, as seen in this mini quilt of mine.

Of course, this space is also wonderful for exploring different quilting options and patterns to add another layer of design to the quilt. Go to the Modern Machine Quilting workshop on page 136 for some great quilting ideas to try.

Composition

In large-scale piecing, one change to either the negative space or the central design can drastically alter the overall composition. When evaluating negative space, the entire layout of the design has to be considered all at once. This can be a difficult shift for some of my students who are more comfortable viewing their composition in smaller sections or in a traditional grid. In a more traditional composition (such as my great-aunt's churn dash quilt on page 129), there is much more wiggle room in the layout of the blocks where changes in their position won't have such a drastic effect on the overall composition; the focus is much more on creating contrast to move the eye across the quilt. This is not the case with large-scale piecing within a large area of negative space. Subtle changes to the positioning of the quilt blocks within the negative space will achieve a completely different look.

Creating Calm

The most important function of negative space in modern quilt making is providing a place for the eye to rest. Negative space should be used to give the composition an area of visual calmness juxtaposed with a more complex quilt block design. This provides focus to the clean lines and the pure

Gelassenheit combines large-scale piecing with both solids and printed fabrics.

color of a design that would likely be lost if large-scale piecing were surrounded with a complex pieced background.

PIECING TIPS AND TECHNIQUES

Fabric Selection

I am a huge fan of solid colored fabrics and advise my students to begin with solids when first trying large-scale piecing. This form of piecing simplifies the overall composition of a quilt, and the use of solid fabrics can reinforce that simplicity and sophistication. Sol-

ids feel painterly to me since they provide large areas of pure color in a quilt, and I feel like I have more control of the overall design when I use solids. With solids, you can choose the exact shade of blue to use with the exact shade of white.

That being said, there are many gorgeous printed fabrics commercially available, and I absolutely feel that they can be used successfully in large-scale piecing as well. See the Working with Prints workshop on page 40 to learn how to create large areas of negative space using prints.

In my large-scale piecing, I find that prints work best in small amounts, so I prefer to use them sparingly.

My Gelassenheit quilt is a great example of how a little print can go a long way. By using a small amount of printed fabric, in such a focused manner, the print really pops against the solid colors in the background.

Fabric Cutting

It is always important to cut fabric accurately, but it is especially so when it comes to large-scale piecing. The best way to ensure accurate cutting is to use a rotary cutter and a straight edge ruler appropriate for the scale of your project. I prefer to use a 60-millimeter rotary cutter and a 6" × 24" clear plastic ruler.

Rulers

Acrylic rulers in a variety of sizes can also aid in accurate fabric cutting. They can be purchased at local quilt shops or even big box fabric retailers and they work well when used with a rotary cutter. My favorite is a 20 ½" square ruler. It's a bit bulky to store in a studio or sewing space, but using a large ruler will help to avoid unnecessary shifting when cutting large-scale pieces.

Fabric Orientation

It is also a good idea to familiarize yourself with cutting fabrics along the length, as opposed to the width, of the fabric when working with large-scale piecing. This method works particularly well with solid fabrics as there are no issues with pattern directionality to accommodate, so the pieces for a project can be cut in any direction to get the required measurements.

Cutting fabric lengthwise also allows you to limit the amount of piecing that is needed to construct a pattern piece that is longer than the typical 42" to 44" width of fabric on a bolt.

Creating Your Work Area

It's also important to have a large work space and cutting area. Because many pattern pieces you will be working with are so much larger than traditional patchwork pieces, it really helps to have the space to achieve accurate cuts. A large cutting area and mat also are useful when cutting fabrics along the length. This way, the yardage can be folded over on top of itself to reduce the length of your cuts. Because you will be cutting through many layers of fabrics, having the room to be able to keep the fabric folded over itself as accurately and smoothly as possible is ideal.

Good Construction

When working with large-scale piecing, mistakes aren't easily hidden, since the overall composition is often simplified. Any inaccurate piecing or unmatched points will be that much more noticeable. Maintain that ¼" seam allowance at all times and be sure your machine is properly adjusted to provide smooth tension.

My sewing room.

EBB AND FLOW

In this design, I have taken a traditional Churn Dash block and expanded it to make it a full 68" square. The results are simple, but striking. Use this technique to refine your color selection and your quilting: when piecing is this large, every small error shows! I provided the Kona colors I used for reference (see right).

FINISHED QUILT SIZE: 73.5" × 73.5"

MATERIALS

4 yards of Fabric 1 (parchment)

¾ yard of Fabric 2 (cadet)

¾ yard of Fabric 3 (artichoke)

4 ¾ yards of backing fabric

5/8 yard of binding fabric

83" × 83" batting

CUTTING THE FABRIC

1. From Fabric 1, cut the following:

☐ One 21" strip. From this, cut one 21" × 21" square (Block A).

☐ Two 11" × 45" strips (Block B).

☐ One 21 ½" strip. From this, cut two 21½" × 21½" squares (Block C).

☐ One 74" strip. From this, cut four 6½" × 74" border strips. Trim two to 6 ½" × 62½" short borders (D). Set aside these and the remaining long border strips (E).

2. From Fabric 2, cut two 10 ½" × 44" strips (Block B).

3. From Fabric 3, cut one 21½" strip. From this, cut two 21½" squares (Block C).

4. From the binding fabric, cut eight 2½" strips.

MAKING THE BLOCKS

1. To make four Block Bs, sew one 10½" × 44" Fabric 1 strip to one 10½" × 44" Fabric 2 strip, right sides together; repeat with the second pair of strips. Press seam open.

From these, cut four 21" × 21" squares.

2. To make four Block Cs, draw a line diagonally from corner to corner on the wrong side of the two 21½" Fabric 1 squares. Then draw a line ¼" on either side of the center line, for a total of three lines.

3. Place one Fabric 1 square and one Fabric 3 square right sides together and pin. Repeat with the other Fabric 1 and Fabric 3 squares. Stitch along the two outer drawn lines on Fabric 1 **(Fig. 1)**.

4. Cut the center lines and press seams open. Repeat with the other Fabric 1 and Fabric 3 squares. Trim all four Block C's to 21" × 21".

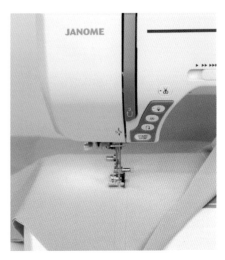

Figure 1

ASSEMBLING THE QUILT

1. To make Row 1 and Row 3, sew two Block Cs on opposite sides of a Block B. Refer to the quilt layout diagram **(Fig. 2)** for color placement. Press seams open. Repeat to make a second row.

2. To make Row 2, sew two Block Bs on opposite sides of Block A. Refer to **Figure 2** for color placement. Press seams open.

3. Sew the rows together. Press the seams open.

4. Following **Figure 2,** sew one D Strip to the top of the quilt top center. Repeat at the bottom. Press seams open.

5. Sew one E Strip to the right and left sides of the quilt top center. Press seams open.

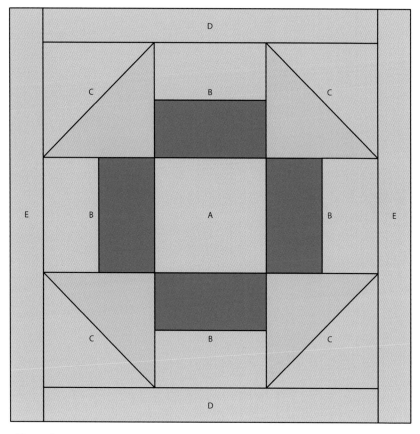

Figure 2

FINISHING THE QUILT

1. Piece the backing fabric to 83" × 83". Press seam open.

2. Layer the backing, batting, and quilt top; baste and quilt as desired. Trim excess backing and batting and square up all sides of the quilt as necessary.

3. Join the binding strips with diagonal seams. Fold the binding strip in half, wrong sides together; press. Bind quilt using a ¼" seam allowance.

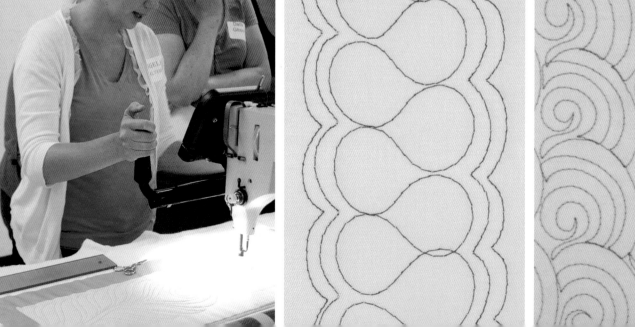

MODERN MACHINE QUILTING

A PRACTICE WORKSHOP

Goal of Class: In this workshop, you'll take simple and sometimes traditional looking quilting designs and learn how to add all the elements needed to make them modern. Following my step-by-step instructions, you will get a feel for how to create unique designs, starting with the design in its simplest form, practicing that movement, then adding minor design elements to achieve a truly custom look in your quilting. I'll teach you four techniques to get you started, but my hope is that you will take what you learn here and use these same minor adjustments to make most any quilting design look great on your modern quilt.

TEACHER:
Angela
Walters

Classic Designs in Modern Quilting

I think that the actual quilting process is the most fun part of quilt making. Depending on your experiences, you may agree with me—or you may be shaking your head. Whether the quilting is your favorite part or not, the fact is that it can enhance, or detract from, the overall look of the quilt in some pretty big ways.

When I started quilting modern quilts, I didn't feel the need to "invent" a new quilting design for each quilt. Instead, I wanted to take the classic machine quilting designs that I loved and use them in different, unexpected ways. In the process I learned how to use echoing, layout, spacing, and combined-design variations to make classic quilting designs perfect for modern piecing.

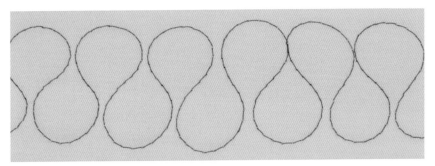

Classic Ribbon Candy.

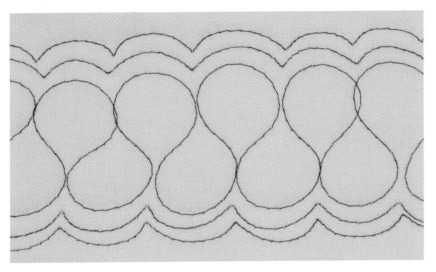

Echoed Ribbon Candy.

WHAT ABOUT THE MACHINE?

"Can I do these designs on my sewing machine?" This is the question I am most often asked. The answer is a loud and resounding "YES!" Even though I use a longarm for most of the quilting I do, all of these designs and variations are easily done on a domestic sewing machine. When it comes to machine quilting, the most important factor to keep in mind is to know where you are going next, no matter what machine is being used.

Now, let's get to the fun part: the quilting!

QUILTER TO QUILTER

There are several other ways to use echoing. Try adding echos when quilting allover designs or use them to highlight motifs, such as feathers.

ECHOING

The first way that you can easily change some of your favorite quilting designs is by echoing them. Echoing is when you outline a previously quilted design a specific distance away. Although echo quilting has been around almost as long as quilting itself, it can add a wonderful modern texture to your quilts. Echoing is a great technique to add to your toolbox because it is completely customizable. You can quilt the echoed lines as closely or as far apart from one another as you feel complements your piecing. You can also add as many echoed lines as you want. When you echo a quilting design, it creates a secondary space that changes the look of the design. For example, I use ribbon candy, a classic machine quilting design, on modern quilt tops all the time.

Tips for Echoing

As much as I love to embellish my quilting designs with echoed lines, it took me a while to become comfortable quilting them. Here are a few tips that really helped me:

1. Keep it consistent...maybe. Personally, I like to keep the echoing consistent in spacing. If I have

A fun example of echoing combined with some traditional designs.

decided on a ½" spacing, I try to keep it that way throughout the quilt. I don't stress too much about it, though, and use the quilting foot on my machine as a guide to keep the spacing consistent. Many of my students like the look of uneven spacing. This varied spacing will give your quilting a completely different look altogether, so be sure to play around with what suits the composition of each pieced top you are quilting.

2. Look to the future: machine quilting is a lot like driving a car;

you want to always be looking ahead of where you are. You should have a plan of where you need to end your stitching for one echo and to begin the next.

3. Practice, practice, practice! Whenever I am teaching a class, I find that the one thing I repeat is "It will get better with practice." This is especially true when it comes to echoing. The more you do it, the more comfortable you will be with it, the more consistent your spacing will be, and the better you will be able to anticipate where to go next.

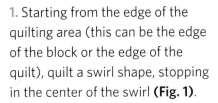
Example of Echoed Flower design.

Figure 1

Figure 2

Figure 3

GIVE IT A TRY:
Echoed Flower Quilting Design

I will show you how to take a classic flower quilting design and make it more modern with a little bit of echoing. This is an easy design to quilt and adds so much texture to the quilt top. It takes a little longer than just quilting a flower design, but the result is so worth it.

1. Starting from the edge of the quilting area (this can be the edge of the block or the edge of the quilt), quilt a swirl shape, stopping in the center of the swirl **(Fig. 1)**.

It doesn't have to be a large swirl, just enough to get you to the center.

2. From the inside, start quilting petals around the swirl, stopping when you run out of room **(Fig. 2)**.

I like to keep all my petals the same shape, usually ¼" to ½".

3. Before adding the next row, echo the petals. Make sure the echoed line is fairly close to the petal. If too far away, it will just look like another row of petals **(Fig. 3)**.

4. Quilt the next row of petals and echo back **(Fig. 4)**.

The mistake that many students make during this step is to try to make the petals touch the middle of the petal below the one they are quilting. Don't worry about that.

TIP

Make sure your swirl is round and not elongated; this will help ensure a circular flower shape.

Figure 4

Figure 5

Figure 6

At this stage, focus on keeping the petals the same size. This means that each petal won't line up with the one below it, but that's okay.

5. Continue adding rows around your flower until you are ready to start a new one. It really doesn't matter how big you make each flower. Once the area is completely quilted, you won't see the individual flowers as much as you see the overall quilted texture.

6. When you are ready to start a new flower, add a partial row of petals to help get you away from the corner or edge or your quilt or block area. Quilt another small swirl **(Fig. 5)**.

7. Repeat the steps above adding rows of petals and echoing them. Again, focus on keeping the spacing between the petals the same.

8. Continue quilting flowers until the area is filled in completely **(Fig. 6)**.

Starting in the center of the block, quilt a small swirl as the center of the flower. Alternate between quilting rows of petals and echoing, just as we did in the steps above.

Want to quilt a classic flower instead of an echoed flower? Follow the steps above, leaving out the echoing in between rows. Now it's your turn! What are some of your favorite designs that you can change up by adding echoing?

TIP

When echoing the petals, you don't have to work your way back to the center of the swirl. Instead stop when you run into the edge of the quilting area or another flower.

When dealing with corners, or areas in which another flower won't fit, echo around previously quilted flowers to fill it in.

Try elongating and echoing swirls for a modern look.

LAYOUT

A little bit of unexpectedness in machine quilting will go a long way. Taking a design and using it in a different way than "normal" is one of my go-to tricks. Not sure what I mean? I promise that all it takes is a little thinking "outside the box". Even though design is perfect for negative space, you can tweak it to use in quilt blocks.

It seems that some machine quilting designs can get typecast into certain roles. One design may be most typically used as an allover design, whereas another design is used only in sashings or blocks. Taking those designs and using them in different areas of the quilt will keep you from getting bored and add a bit of modern fun to your quilt.

For instance, consider the Classic Swirl design. Swirls are normally used as an allover design, but what if you quilted them in rows instead of random directions? What if you elongated the swirl (see above).

The result is a design that would work well in many areas of a quilt.

But why stop there? What if you broke the swirls apart and used them in the border, or sashing, of a quilt?

Think Outside the "Quilting" Box

1. Try making the layout more regulated to get a different look?

2. Try taking a component of a quilting design you may have already integrated and use it in a different area of the quilt?

3. Where is this design normally used? Try using it in a completely different area of a quilt.

Try quilting swirls in the borders of your quilt.

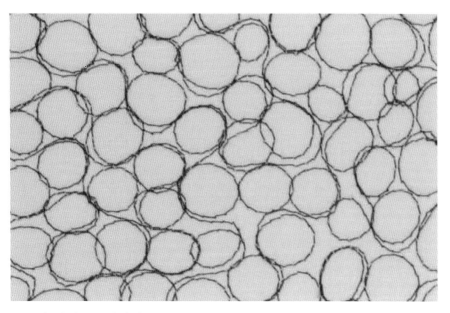

Example of Classic Pebble design.

Figure 1

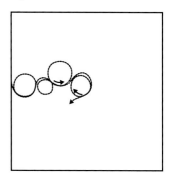

Figure 2

GIVE IT A TRY: Overlapping Pebbles

Pebbles are a staple in machine quilting. They can pull double duty as a filler design as well as be used as a way to highlight specific areas of your quilt. Try quilting this design in different sizes to really change up the look.

Pebbles

As long as pebbles, or circles, have been around, the goal seems to have been to make them consistent in size and layout. One of the first things I was taught about quilting the pebble design was that they were never, supposed to cross over one another! Well, in this section, we are going to break the rules.

Before we get started on the Overlapping Pebbles variation, let's practice the fundamentals of the Classic Pebble design, a great option for all-over quilting.

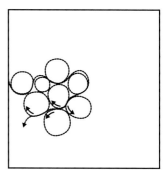

Figure 3

1. Quilt a circle and, without stopping, change direction and quilt another circle. almost like a figure eight **(Fig. 1)**.

2. Quilt another circle, again changing direction so that it is touching the circle you just quilted **(Fig. 2)**.

3. Continue filling in the quilting area by quilting circles, trying to get them as close to each other as possible **(Fig. 3)**.

Even though pebbles are normally quilted in consistent sizes, try

changing the size to get a different look! Next, I'll show you a variation I call "Overlapping Pebbles."

This design looks great in all areas of a quilt. From borders to blocks, overlapping pebbles will add a fun and modern texture to your quilt. It works best when quilted in a slightly larger scale than classic pebbles.

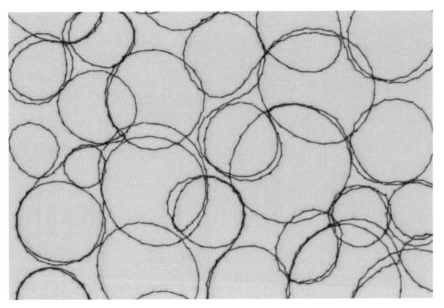

Example of Overlapping Pebbles.

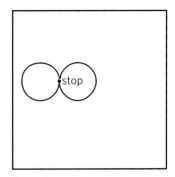

Figure 1

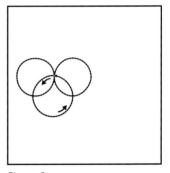

Figure 2

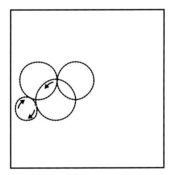

Figure 3

Modern Variation

1. Quilt two circles, just like you would with Classic Pebbles. Stop when you are at a point where the two pebbles touch **(Fig. 1)**.

2. From that point, quilt a circle that overlaps the first two circles **(Fig. 2)**.

3. Continue around the circle until you are out of the first two circles and quilt another circle that touches the previously quilted circle **(Fig. 3)**.

4. Repeat the steps above until you have filled the whole quilting area.

Now it's your turn! Which of your favorite designs could you recast into a different layout?

QUILTER TO QUILTER

This design looks best when you alternate between touching circles and overlapping circles. If all the circles overlap, it will look messy.

This quilting plays with the line spacing within a design.

SPACING

Even though we each might need our "personal space," the same isn't always true for our favorite quilting designs. In this section, I will show you how adjusting the spacing in your quilting designs can yield some great results.

The "spacing" of a design can refer to a couple of different things. It can be the spacing between the lines within the design (for example, the spaces between the petals of a flower in a Flower Meander) or it can be the distance between the individual components of a design (for example, the distance between the individual flowers in a Flower Meander).

Within Designs

Let's look at the Square Chain: a geometric quilting design that works great in borders. Normally, I would keep the spacing of the lines within the square squares consistent **(Fig. 1)**. But if I wanted a more fun, funkier twist, I could vary the spacing of those lines **(Fig. 2)**.

Figure 1

Between Designs

Varying the spacing between individual designs is yet another way you can tweak your favorite quilting design. Let's take another look at the Square Chain design. When quilting the design, you can quilt the squares so that they are close and orderly **(Fig. 1)**.

Now let's look at the design when we change up the spacing between the squares **(Fig. 2)**.

This tweak doesn't take any longer to quilt, and it gives the design a fresh look. When quilting this sample, I quilted the squares and spaced them out, then fit the next row of squares in the empty spaces.

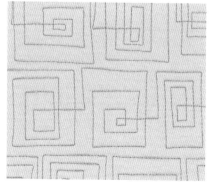

Figure 2

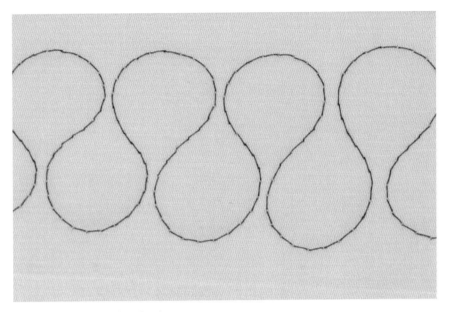

Example of Classic Ribbon Candy.

GIVE IT A TRY: Ribbon Candy Variation

When I first started machine quilting, I had a tough time learning the classic Ribbon Candy design. As soon as I thought that I had it figured out, I would start to mess up. If you are struggling with the classic version, jump right to the variation. It's a little more forgiving. No matter which one you choose, it will look great on your quilts.

Ribbon Candy

Ribbon Candy is a classic design that I frequently use. It's great for smaller borders and sashing, but by adjusting the spacing, this design can easily be used in larger areas. Before I get too ahead of myself, let's talk about the classic Ribbon Candy design:

1. Starting from the edge, quilt a backward S shape **(Fig. 1)**.

2. Without stopping, quilt the same shape in reverse, so that the rounded sides almost touch **(Fig. 2)**.

3. Repeat this motion until your desired area is completely quilted **(Fig. 3)**.

Now, let's change up the spacing. When students want to use the ribbon candy design in wider sashings and borders, I ask them to scoot the main design closer together so that the overall effect doesn't look too spread out. I will admit that it took me awhile to get used to quilting it this way, but with practice, I am sure you will pick it up in no time.

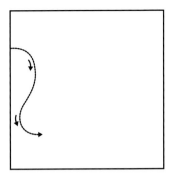

Figure 1

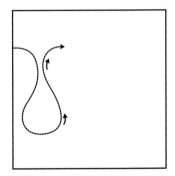

Figure 2

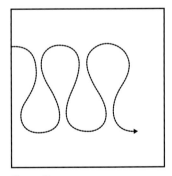

Figure 3

TIP

Try to keep the design from touching the edge of the quilting area, keeping it about ⅛" away. This will help make sure you don't lose the round top and bottom in the seam.

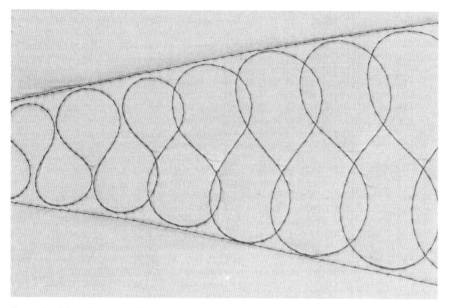

Example of Overlapping Ribbon Candy within an irregular block shape.

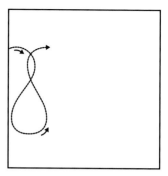

Figure 1

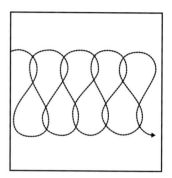

Figure 2

Modern Variation

1. Just as you did in the Classic Ribbon Candy, quilt a backward S. The trickiest thing about the ribbon candy design is getting used to the motion of reversing direction. Try drawing it out beforehand to get the hang of it. Without stopping, quilt the reverse shape so that it crosses over the rounded part of the first one **(Fig. 1)**.

2. Continue quilting, trying to keep the spacing consistent **(Fig. 2)**.

This variation also works great in irregular shaped blocks and areas of your quilt. In the skinnier areas, quilt the classic Ribbon Candy, slowly evolving to the ribbon candy variation in the wider areas.

Now it's your turn!

The next time you are getting ready to quilt your favorite design, ask yourself how, by simply adjusting the spacing, you can achieve a more modern design for your quilt.

QUILTER TO QUILTER

Varying the spacing of your quilting designs will not only change the look: it will determine the density of the quilting. Quilting the designs more closely will result in denser quilting and vice versa.

Many designs are incorporated in this example but work well overall.

COMBINING DESIGNS

Combing quilting designs is probably the only time where 1 + 1 = 3. Taking two of your favorite quilting designs and combining them to create a third design is not only fun: it's easy. This section will get your mind whirling with ideas and soon no quilting design will be safe!

When it comes to combining quilting designs, you will find that some shapes work better together than others. Designs that have the same basic shape usually blend well together, such as Classic Pebbles and Swirls (which I'll show you how to do later in this section). Some designs are super friendly and work fantastic with most designs; for instance, Classic Pebbles and Paisleys are two designs that are easily combined with other designs. If you have two quilting designs that you are just itching to quilt together, try sketching it out on paper first. Usually, if they play well together on paper, they will quilt together well.

So Many Different Ways

When it comes to combining quilting designs, there is more than just one way to go about it.

The Straight Forward Approach
Throw two different designs together and see what happens.

Why stop at just two quilting designs when three can be so much more fun? Try several different designs for an even more custom look. For example, you can throw Swirls, Classic Pebbles and Flowers together.

Mixed Up
Instead of throwing them together, incorporate two or more designs in a truly intertwined way. The Swirl variation given on page 150 shows how to do just that.

Example of Modern Swirls.

GIVE IT A TRY: Swirls Variation

If there was an award for the most versatile quilting design, it would have to go to Swirls! They work well on all sorts of quilts. From traditional to modern, from pieced to appliqué. I have used them as an all-over design, as a filler and even as a way to break up large areas of negative space. They are also very easy to combine with other designs to create even more possibilities.

Classic Swirls

Because Swirls are so versatile, they look great on almost any quilt. In this section, I will show you how combining Classic Pebbles and Swirls can give your quilt a custom look. This design can be used as an allover design, in negative space, or in larger quilt blocks. You can also easily change up the scale to suit your preferences. But first, let me show you how to make the Classic Swirl.

1. From the edge of the quilting area, quilt a Swirl, leaving ½" to ¾" spacing between the lines **(Fig. 1)**.

2. From the center, quilt your way back out, stopping when you touch the edge of the quilting area or another Swirl **(Fig. 2)**.

3. Travel along the edge of the quilting area approximately ½" and Echo around the outside of the Swirl **(Fig. 3)**.

Figure 1

Figure 2

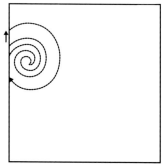

Figure 3

TIP

This is a fun way to practice quilting designs that you aren't completely comfortable with. Throwing a design in randomly allows you to get a feel for it, without committing to quilting the design over a larger portion of the quilt.

Example of random Pebbles within Swirls.

Figure 1

Figure 2

Modern Variation

1. Just as you did for the steps for the Classic Swirl, make a swirl leaving larger spaces between your echoes. Making this area wider will help you fit in the Classic Pebbles more easily. This time, quilt circles in between the Swirl and the Echo you just quilted **(Fig. 1)**.

2. Echo around the Swirl again, this time only ¼" away **(Fig. 2)**.

When quilting these kinds of Swirls, I like how it looks with an Echo on each side of the Classic Pebbles. It's purely a personal preference though.

3. When ready to start another Swirl, travel ½" to 1" along the edge of the Swirl that you just quilted. Quilt another Swirl so that it touches the first Swirl **(Fig. 3)**.

4. Repeat the steps above to continue quilting Swirls and Classic Pebbles until the quilting area is filled **(Fig. 4)**.

If you don't want to take the time to quilt Classic Pebbles in all your Swirls, just add Classic Pebbles into random swirls or use this type of Swirl in select areas of your quilt.

Figure 3

Figure 4

THE SKY'S THE LIMIT

I hope that this chapter has you eager to try different ideas. The tips and examples I have shared in this workshop aren't mutually exclusive; try using them together. For instance, try combining designs and echoing them. Or try adjusting the spacing of a design and using it in a different layout. Regardless of the quilting designs you use or how you quilt your quilt, the most important goal of this workshop is to encourage you to have fun with your quilting and try something new, modern, and unexpected. Happy Quilting!

QUILTER TO QUILTER

You can overlap the designs as much as you would like, depending how large the quilting area is. Sometimes, I will overlap the designs by only ¼". Other times, I will overlap them even more. Play with the design until you find your comfort zone.

A STUDY OF MODERN QUILTS

A DESIGN WORKSHOP

Goal of the Class: Often times, the best way to learn is by example. In this gallery workshop, I have selected fifty of the most compelling modern quilts to help you both understand some of the design principles discussed in other workshops, and to inspire you to create your own unique designs. Because many of the fast-paced social media tools we enjoy today leave us with fleeting impressions and a craving for the new and the next, this gallery is also a wonderful opportunity to document where modern quilt making has come from, and what we are making today.

TEACHER:
Heather Grant

A Study of 50 Modern Quilts

I started quilting in 1995. I was barely in my twenties but it was one the only crafts that always appealed to me. When I started to become attracted to mid-century style, the quilting at the time was at the other end of the style spectrum. I stopped quilting.

I was working at a book wholesaler in 2002 and ran across a copy of Yoshiko Jinzenji's book Quilt Artistry. Wonder and amazement came over me as I thumbed through the pages. I was shocked that quilting could work with mid-century modern design.

It was then I started up quilting again.

In 2007, I posted one of my quilts on a message board and Rossie Hutchinson invited me to her Flickr group, Fresh Modern Quilts. I was no longer alone, because in this group I found other quilters who liked the same style. When the Modern Quilt Guilds started popping up, I started a guild in Austin, Texas.

In 2010, I started to find there was an conflicting messages online on what was modern. It was clear to me, but I wanted to communicate it in a positive way. I started my blog, Modern Day Quilts, to showcase the quilts I thought were modern. In a way, I was a critic by omission.

Many people have many different definitions of modern quilting. My own definition has evolved from when I first was invited to Rossie's Flickr group. However, I find the definition is helpful to our work and helps the evolution and design process of modern quilting.

I often compare design elements like improvisational piecing, minimalism, expansive negative space, scale, alternate grid work and color as being ingredients in a salad bar. You could pile it all on your plate, but you may not have a great salad. When composing your quilt, pick and choose from the design element salad bar. Two or three design elements used together can make an amazing quilt.

I hope this gallery will inspire you when making your own quilt salad. They all contain some of these modern quilt design elements, but when used in different ways, make much different quilts.

DOUBLE EDGED LOVE

Victoria Findlay Woolfe
quilted by Lisa Sipes
66" x 76"
A lot of the work I do is based on traditional patterns so I am always asking myself " how can I sustain the integrity of a traditional pattern yet update it with energy and imagination?" This quilt explores that and is also a study of where I came from and where I am now. My grandmother was the quilter who inspired my creative process and I am grateful for that past.
bumblebeansinc.com

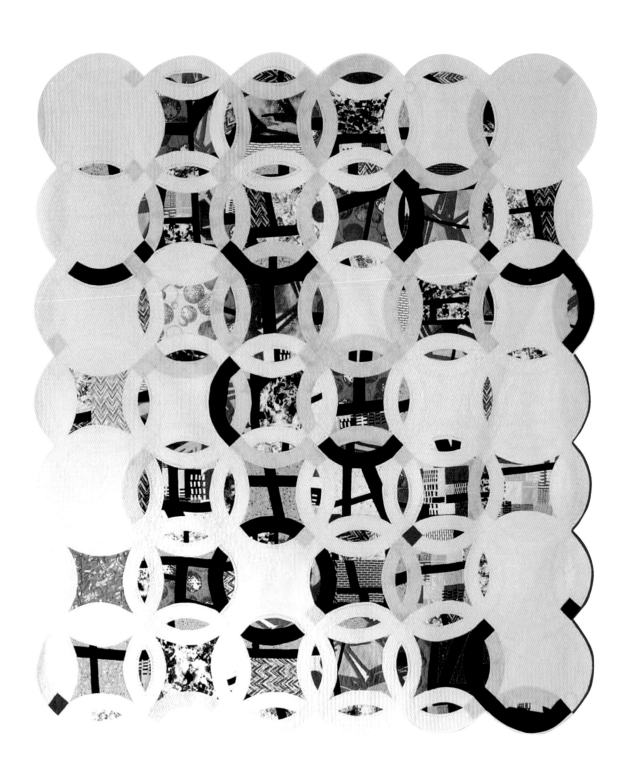

TANGELO

Carolyn Friedlander

68" x 72"

A fan of gradations, I thought of backgammon boards to create blurred triangular shapes across the quilt. I used a single background color and stripes of prints that bleed into the background before changing to the next color.
carolynfriedlander.com

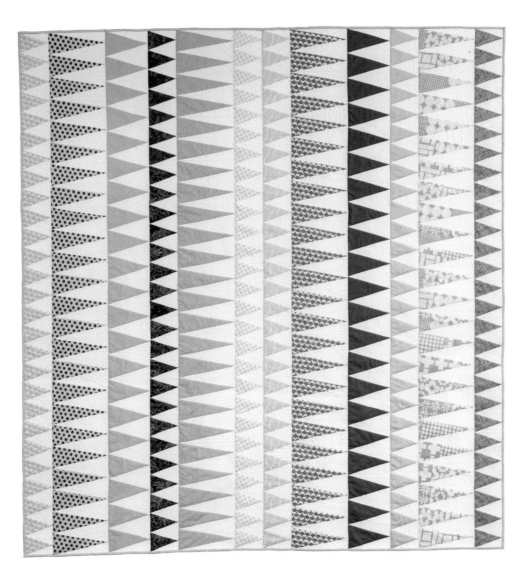

SEA GLASS HERRINGBONE

Claire Jain

29" x 60"

This is a herringbone pattern made without half-square triangles. I was inspired by the color palette that Kati Spencer used in a quilt she shared on the Lily's Quilts blog.
sewingoverpins.com

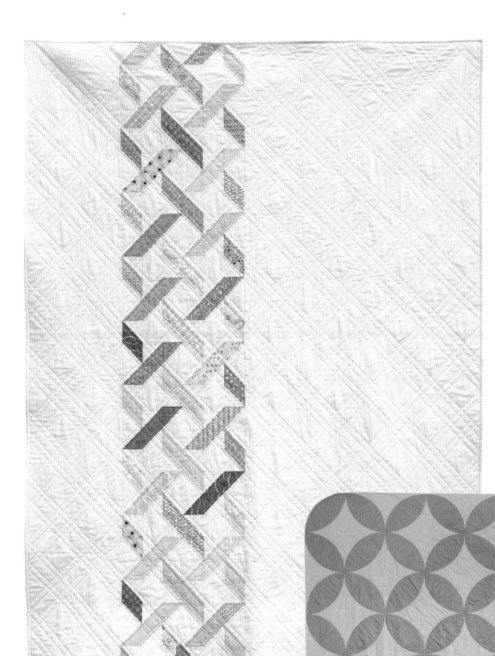

DIAMOND TREAD

Lee Heinrich

52" x 75"

Half-square triangles mimic the look of "diamond tread" patterned steel. I added negative space on either side for more impact which looks like a truck ran right over it.
freshlypieced.com

ORANGE PEEL

Elizabeth Ancell

90" x 90"

Originally created as a small digital image I used for making paper goods like envelopes, it was only a matter of time before I converted the design into a quilt!
flickr.com/photos/elizabeth_ancell

MOD BEADS

Liz Harvatine

45" x 60"

I wanted to explore ways of getting curves into my quilts. I made pattern pieces on the computer that enabled me to make very precise shapes.

ladyharvatine.com

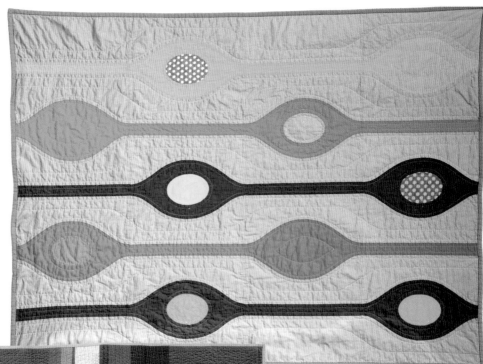

THE GREEN QUILT

Rossie Hutchinson

Quilted by Bernie Olszewski

50" x 56"

I pieced this improvisationally, using a design by Denyse Schmidt as inspiration. I overdyed some commercial fabrics, experimenting in mixing itajime with modern quilt practices.

r0ssie.blogspot.com

3/4 LOG CABIN

Ara Jane Olufson

48" x 60"

This quilt was made with blocks from my online charity quilting bee, the Love Circle of Do Good Stitches. The blocks appear to be different sizes when stacked randomly, but are identical sizes. *whatarajaneloves. blogspot.com*

SOMEWHERE UNDER

Jessica Levitt

54" x 65"

Inspired by an abstract painting, this pattern has a quirky, handmade feel. The piecing is intentionally just a little crooked and the quilting is all done freehand. *juicy-bits.typepad.com*

AFTERMATH

Jacquie Gering

41" x 60"

This quilt was inspired by the television images of the Boston Marathon bombing when only trash and bloodstains remained. In all acts of violence there is aftermath, both positive and negative, and in that aftermath remains work to be done, help to be offered, and ongoing care and changes to be made. This quilt is a reminder to continue to do what I can.

tallgrassprairiestudio.blogspot.com

CROSS IT

Brigette Heitland

84" x 84"

Have you ever played Pick Up Sticks? This game calms me down and helps me concentrate – just like this quilt. The clean lines and colors exude a quiet, focused energy while the large frame and delicate center provide balance.

bheitland.wix.com

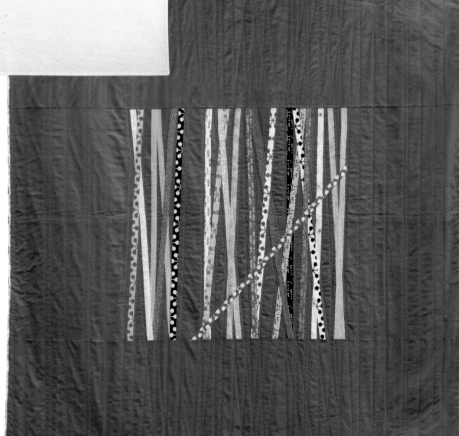

SKY.MO.AUGUST

Kim Eichler-Messmer

31" x 56"

I use a combination of planned and improv piecing to represent the sky and land. I am interested in capturing and abstracting qualities of light that occur in the Midwest.

kimemquilts.com

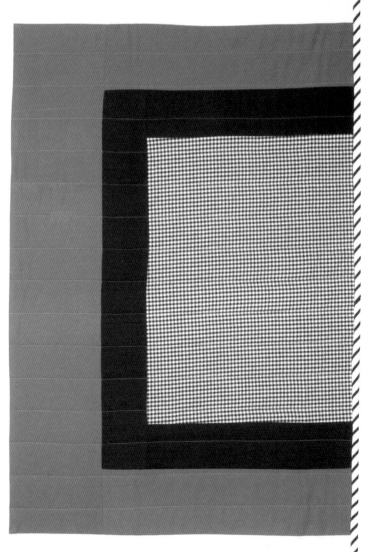

LITTLE BLUE COURTHOUSE

Hopewell Workshop

30" x 40"

The design stems from the studio's New Courthouse quilt, which combines the work of Josef Albers and a traditional courthouse quilting pattern.

hopewell.com

LIBRARY STEPS

Season Evans

70" x 82"

Library Steps is based on the courthouse steps block. The prominent negative space is used to highlight the simplicity of the traditional pattern. *sdequilts.com*

Photo Credit: Meagan West

BIAS 2

Alissa Haight Carlton

60" x 75"

This quilt explores straight lines on the bias. I emphasized the negative space by piecing the binding to match the quilt top, which extends the lines off the frame. *handmadebyalissa.com*

MODERN CHEVRON BABY QUILT

Kirsty Cleverly

45" x 60"

Inspired by the pattern on a manhole cover, I spent an afternoon with graph paper and a calculator to design a scale I liked before tackling the measurments.
bonjourquilts.com

UNTITLED QUILT #7

Sarah Nishiura

72" x 92"

Inspired by one of my favorite patterns "streak of lightening", this design traditionally involves piecing many long narrow zig zag lines. I enlarged the motif to create one giant zig zag.
sarahnishiura.com

TRICHISEL

Heather Scrimsher

45" x 50"

I used a traditional block and transformed it. Each row is slightly different, creating a sampler. I call it the Tri-Chisel, which I then reduced to "Trichisel".

fiberosity.com

CONTACT C

Jen Carlton Bailly, quilted by Nancy Stovall of Just Quilting

72" x 72"

I designed this quilt while nursing a cold. Remember those cold pills with the little beads inside? I'm not sure if it was the fever or the cold medicine but that is exactly what this quilt turned into!

bettycrockerass.com

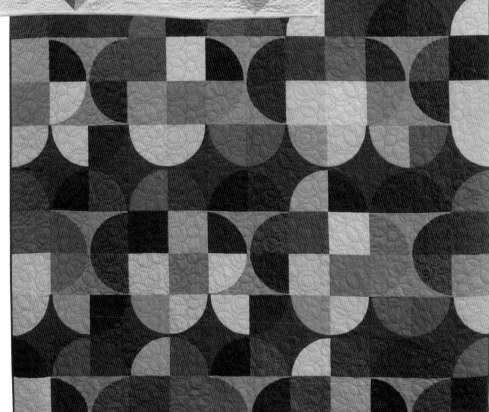

BIG HEX

Andres Rosales

53" x 49"

My first hexagon quilt is made of one large hexagon to create a strong visual impact. I improvisationally cut and pieced the color strips then cut the six triangles out using a custom template.

madtesla.com

LESS IS MORE

Elizabeth Dackson

56" x 70"

Flipping the traditional block on point creates an eye-catching X shape. The X is emphasized by using different color values of solids throughout the blocks.

dontcallmebetsy.com

Photo Credit: From Becoming a Confident Quilter by Elizabeth Dackson. Published Fall 2013 by Martingale. Photo by Brent Kane.

OMBRE
DUTCHMAN

Vanessa Christensen

48" x 48"

Individual block shapes and intrecate piecing details can often be lost when too much patterned fabric is used. By concentrating on solids, the block shapes and details are more clear.

vanessachristenson.com

STAR'D

Kristy Daum

50" x 60"

For a MQG Challenge, we modernized the Ohio Star. I subtracted a key component from the traditional block with each rendition. The Flying Geese help move your eye around the quilt.

stlouisfolkvictorian. blogspot.com

PARTLY CLOUDY

Alexandra Ledgerwood

40" x 50"

A scrappy interpretation of a coin quilt, this design uses a limited color palette to provide cohesion. Using rectangular blocks keeps the gradation choppy and graphic.

teaginnydesigns.blogspot.com

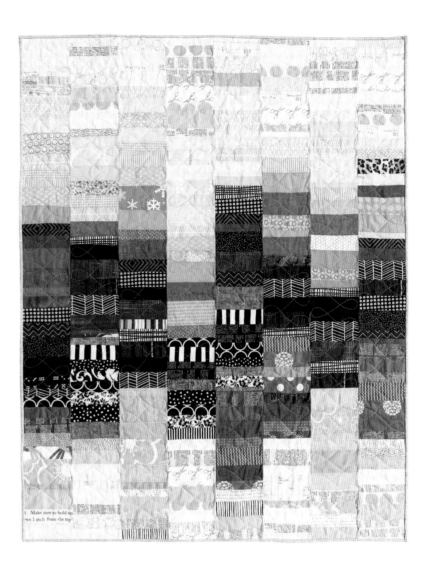

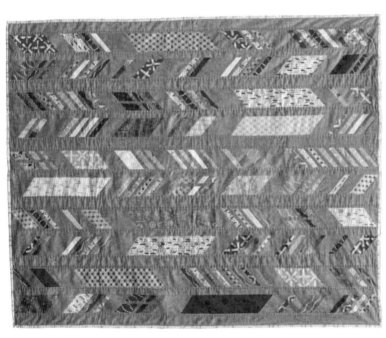

FEATHERS

Alison Glass,

pattern by
Alison Glass and
Nydia Kehnle

44" x 55"

Based on a fabric I created as part of my Sun Print collection for Andover Fabrics, Nydia Kehnle and I co-designed this flexible paper pieced pattern to allow for many possible arrangements.

alisonglass.com

ANNI

Heather Jones

100" x 100"

I was inspired by Josef Albers' series of works titled "Homage to the Square," where he experimented with the relationships between different colors arranged in a series of squares.

oliveandollie.com

DARK BERRY BOLD

Barbara Perrino

32" x 36"

This is a minimal interpretation of the Log Cabin design. Open rectangular shapes, alternating in color, are siutated horizontally and vertically. The gray binding fabric unexpectedly unifies the palette.

bperrino.com

KISS KISS
Cheryl Arkison
Sep-13, 105″ x 90″
When writing XO, which is a hug and which is a kiss? My husband thinks the X is a hug and the O is a kiss. Nine improv pieced Xs and pebble quilted Os settle the debate.
cherylarkison.com

GRAPHIC GIRL
Elizabeth Ancell
40" x 47"
I designed the Graphic Girl Quilt pattern was using one piece of gray fabric and used a technique similar to Dale Fleming's six-minute circle to construct it.
flickr.com/photos/ elizabeth_ancell

BLOOM

Carson Converse

39" x 51"

Interested in reinterpreting the Diamond Within a Square in a modern way, I adjusted the scale and placed the blocks in an organic arrangement.

carsonconverse.com

STICKS AND STONES

Rachel (2nd Ave Studio)

36" x 42"

This quilt is an homage to Eames. Instead of quickly fusing some shapes or employing raw edge appliqué, I hand turned the edges.

2ndavenuestudio.blogspot.com

Photo Credit: Rachel I Kerley @ 2nd Ave Studio

IDAHO
Maura Ambrose
90" x 90"
The X design was inspired by the mountainous state of Idaho. I dyed the fabrics individually to create an intentional shift in color tone by using a few different pomegranate dye baths.
folkfibers.com

MODERN CABIN
Leslie Schmidt
65" x 82"
An art teacher once told me, "There are no ugly colors, just unfortunate combinations." This quilt marries two super-saturated colors and achieves balance without subordinating the intensity of either.
amidwesternnewyorker. blogspot.com

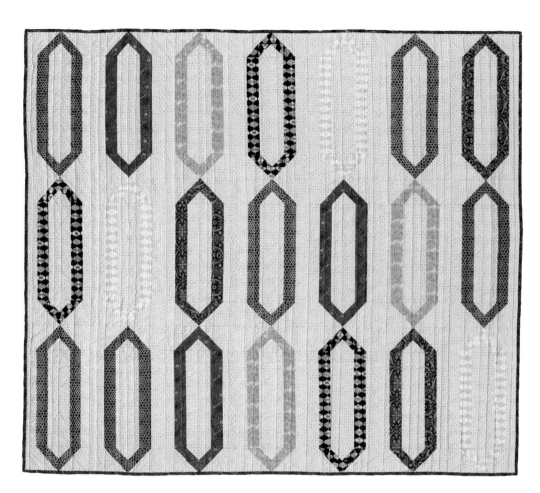

BUTTONHOLES

Amy Ellis, quilted by
Natalie Bonner

54" x 63"

By alternating the fabric placement and adding linear quilting, these traditional flying-geese units have a modern look.

amyscreativeside.com

SCIENCE FAIR

Julie Herman of Jaybird Quilts

48" x 65"

I designed the layout to play up the use of positive and negative space, with the negative space featuring more prominently in the design.

jaybirdquilts.com

UNTITLED QUILT #16

Sarah Nishiura

46" x 40"

This quilt was the result of a casual doodle - two lines crisscrossing and constrained by the rectangle that contains them.
sarahnishiura.com

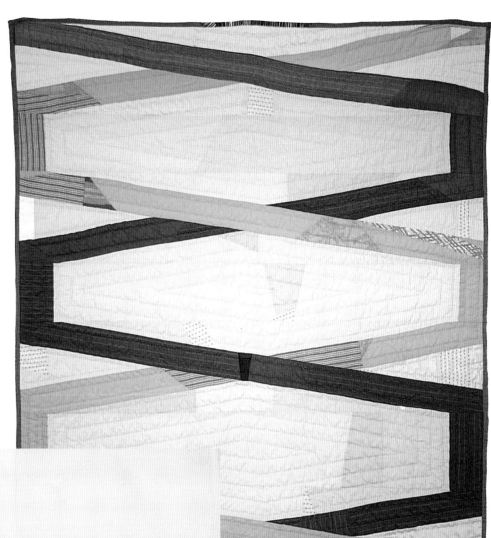

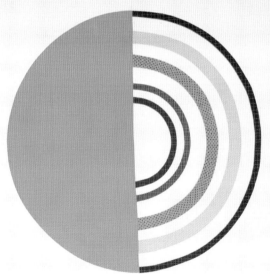

THE BIG O

Latifah Saafir

54" x 65"

The Big "O" is the second quilt in a series celebrating the O. It uses machine bias tape applique and the Pinless Piecing technique developed by Dale Fleming.
thequiltengineer.com

GRAVITY
Season Evans
44" x 60"

Based on the traditional roman stripes block, these blocks are inverted and mirrored to create vertical movement.

sdequilts.com

Photo Credit: Meagan West

TO THE POINT
Amy Ellis, quilted by Natalie Bonner
60" x 72"

Thoughtfully placed triangles and rectangles create a dynamic secondary pattern. The solid fabric and linear quilting each add an interesting layer to the design.

amyscreativeside.com

Photo Credit: From Modern Basics II by Amy Ellis, Martingale, 2013; used by permission. Photo by Brent Kane. All rights reserved.

UNTITLED

Lindsey Stead

60" x 60"

I focused on the process of subtraction within grey components to create a pattern that is largely comprised of negative space. Using only two neutral colors, the asymmetrical design creates a unique variation of the Log Cabin.

lindsaystead.com

INTERSECTIONS

Alissa Haight Carlton

60" x 75"

Just two contrasting fabrics were used to create this quilt. Dense straight-line quilting to fill in the negative space contributes to the graphic nature of this design.

handmadebyalissa.com

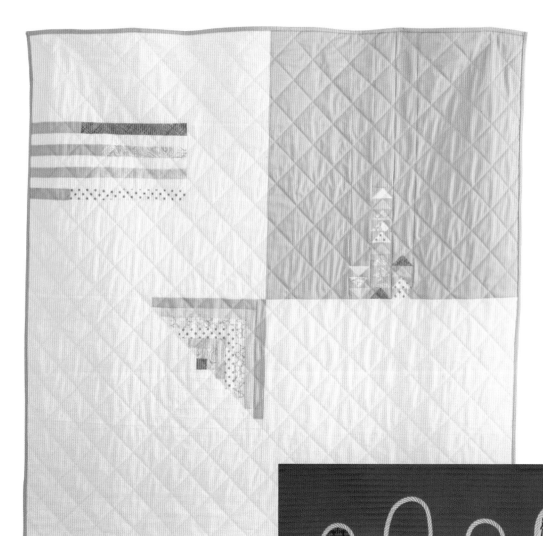

SIMPLE FOUR SQUARE

Purl Soho

48" x 48"

I'm not a painter, but I imagine that quilt making is similar. This quilt explores the color and proportionality of block patterns in an unorthodox way, much like a painting.

purlsoho.com

AIRSHOW

Latifah Saafir

45" x 45"

Through my love of making bias tape, I was inspired to create this bold quilt where bias tape was used as the focus of the design.

thequiltengineer.com

LINEN PINWHEEL

Barbara Perrino

33" x 41"

This quilt is an exercise in the "less is more" approach to design in regard to both line and palette. Cool and neutral tones set against the angles, imbue the piece with quiet contrast.

bperrino.com

THIS WAY, THAT WAY

Faith Jones, Fresh Lemons Quilts

30" x 40"

This is an improvisationally pieced flying geese pattern using foundation paper which made working with the linen easy.

freshlemonsquilts.com

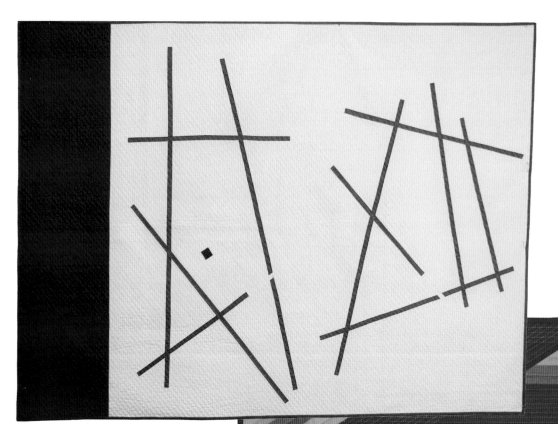

UNPARELLEL
Jacquie Gering
43" x 58"
Made using the slice and insert technique, this design was inspired by a metal sculpture. I love the high contrast between the background and the lines. *tallgrassprairiestudio. blogspot.com*

HELIX
Nicole Neblett
23" x 29"
This minimal design works with three colors alternated in strips and is quilted using straight lines following the angles. The overlapping strips remind me of a DNA helix. *mamalovesquilts. blogspot.com*

FLY BY NIGHT

Kevin Kosbab

40" x 42"

The idea for this design came while circling the airport waiting for many planes to land. The simple, abstract piecing adds movement, but the echo quilting really lets the airplane shapes take flight.

feeddog.net

Photo Credit: © 2014 Kevin Kosbab/Feed Dog Designs

FRACTAL RADIANCE

Katie Larson

pattern by Katie Larson for the Kansas City MQG

62" x 86"

The irregular triangles were too large for paper piecing so I calculated the triangle dimensions and then transferred them onto the fabric. This pattern is fundraiser for the Kansas City MQG.

kcmodernquiltguild. blogspot.

Photo Credit: Sarah Sorrell

Templates

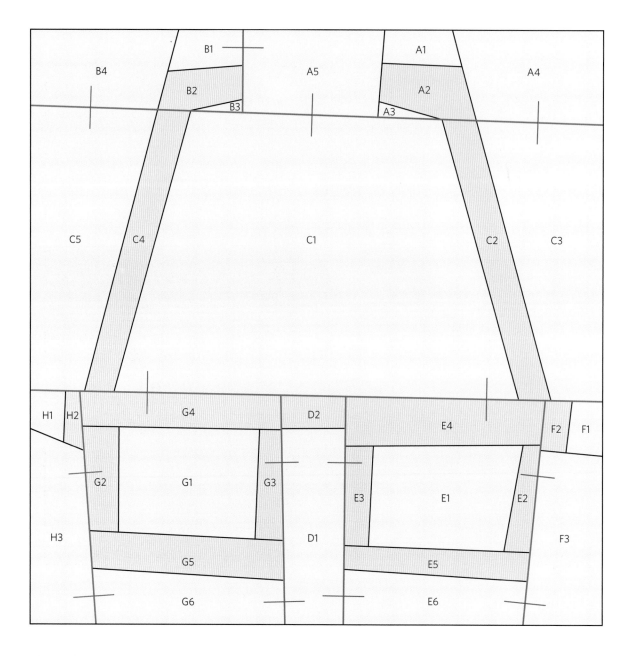

ENLARGE 120%

FINAL SIZE 7¾" x 7¾"

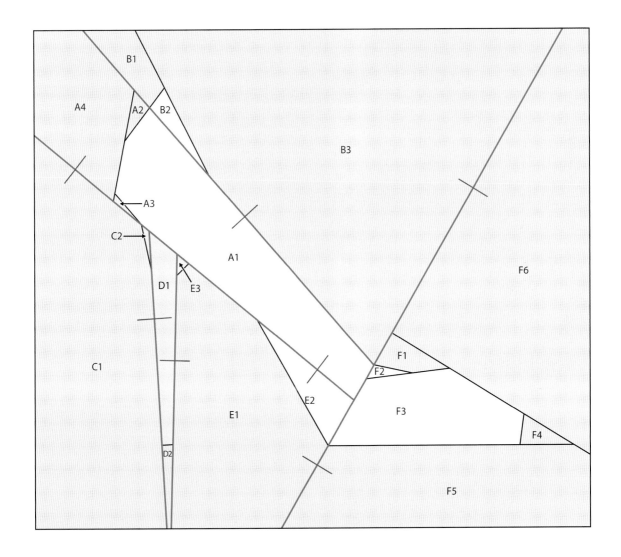

ENLARGE 120%
FINAL SIZE 6½" x 7 ½"

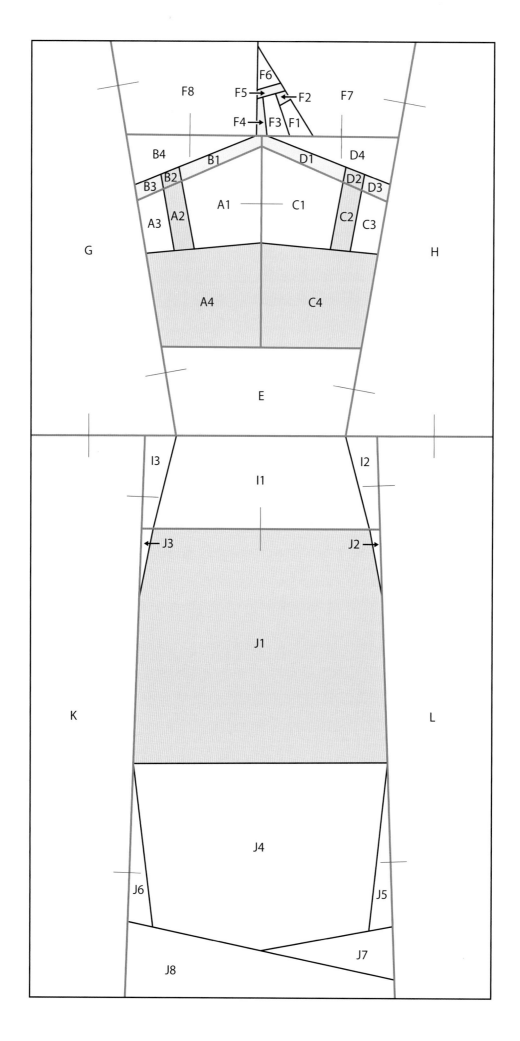

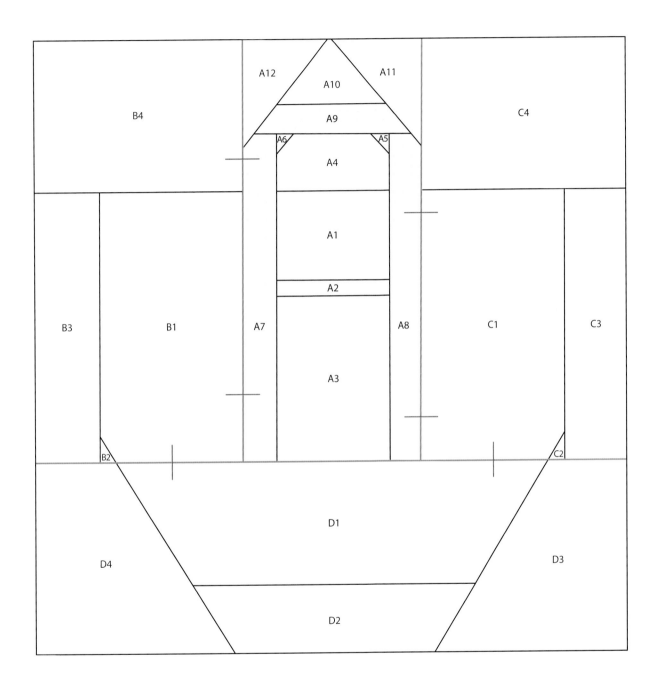

ENLARGE 120%
FINAL SIZE 8"x 8"

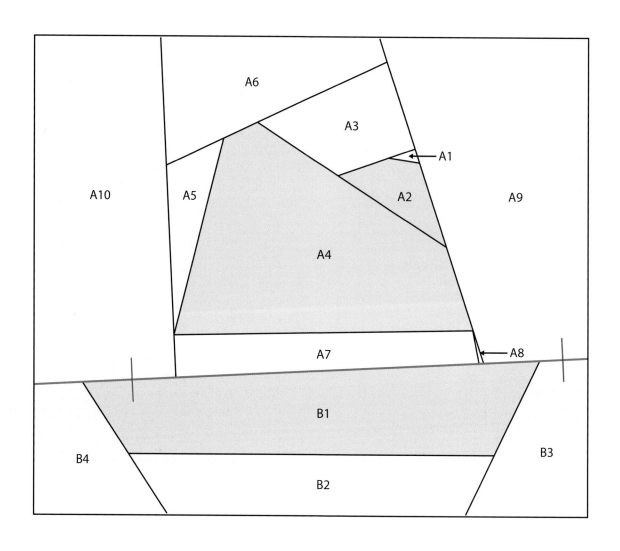

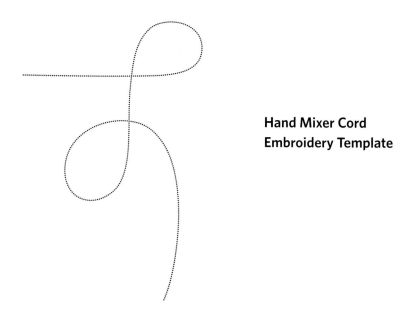

**Hand Mixer Cord
Embroidery Template**

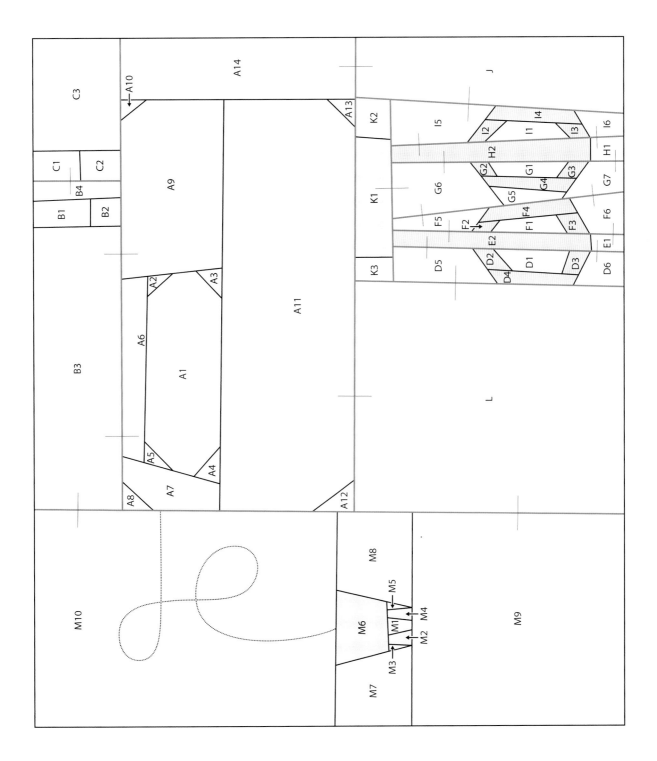

ENLARGE 120%

FINAL SIZE 8"x 9"

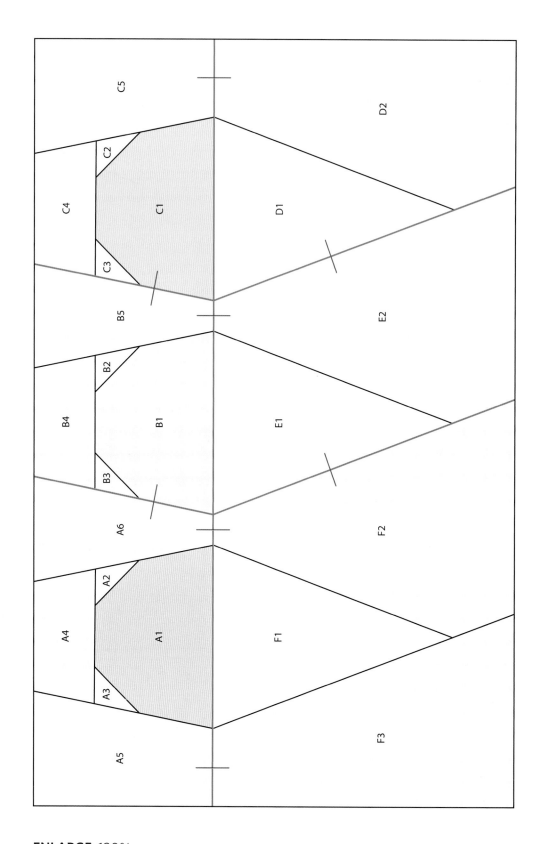

ENLARGE 120%

FINAL SIZE 6½"x 10"

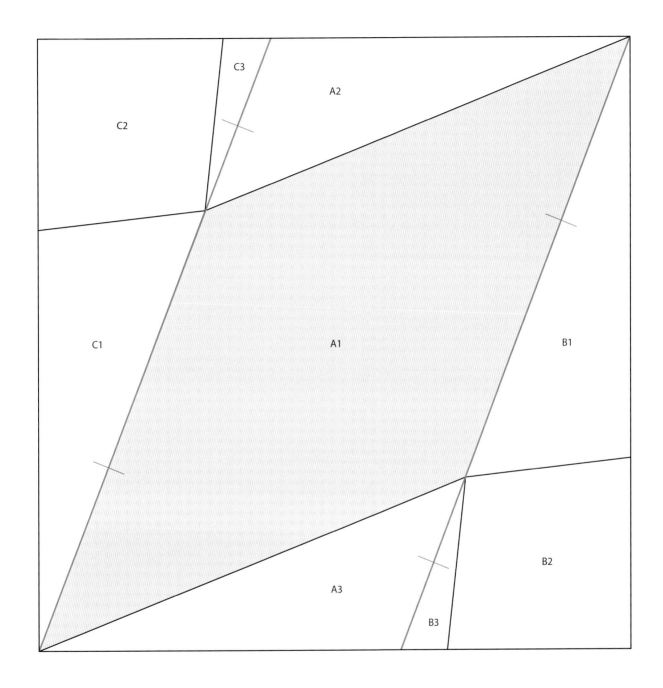

ENLARGE 120%

FINAL SIZE 8"x 8"

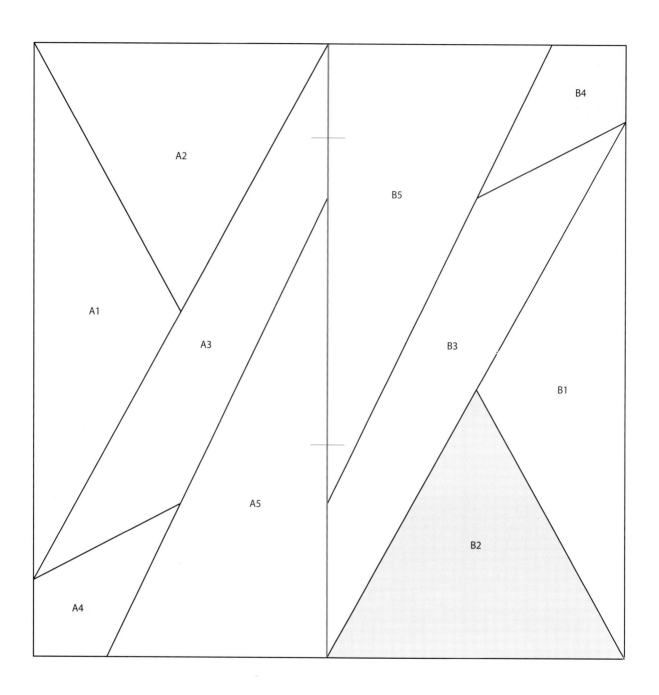

ENLARGE 120%
FINAL SIZE 8"x 8"

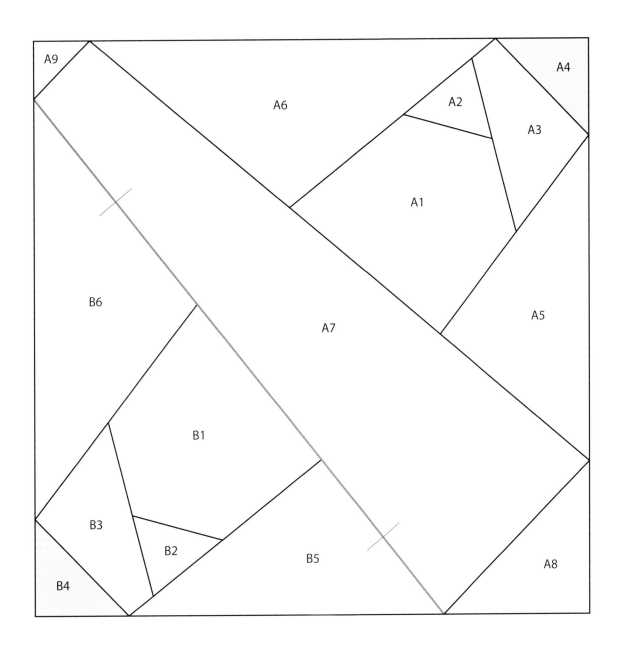

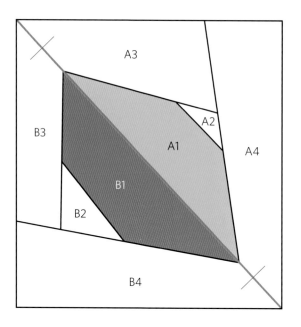

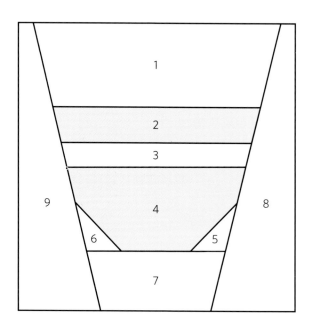

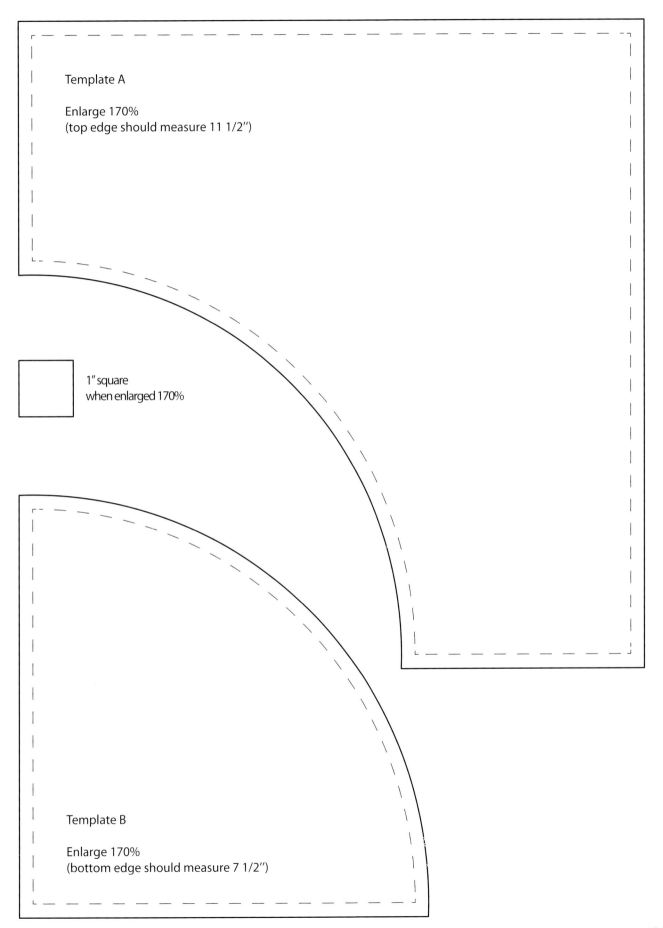

Template A

Enlarge 170%
(top edge should measure 11 1/2″)

1″ square
when enlarged 170%

Template B

Enlarge 170%
(bottom edge should measure 7 1/2″)

12/23

Photo Credits

© **Erin Cox Photography** pages 3, 6, 24, 40, 62, 82, 124, 192.

© **Gale Zucker Photography** pages 4, 44, 45, 52-61.

© **Lucky Spool Media, LLC** pages 8-18, 20, 26-28, 33, 34, 42, 46, 49, 50, 76, 85- 106, 108-116, 120-122, 132, 134, 138, 140, 143, 144, 146, 147, 149.

© **Andrew Kowalyshyn,** photo of Kari Vojtechovsky, page 7.

© **Rossie Hutchinson,** photo of Daniel Rouse, page 40.

© **Alissa Haight Carlton,** photo of Jacquie Gering, page 62.

© **Kate Inglis,** photo of Cheryl Arkison, page 83.

© **Melissa Lytle,** photo of Penny Layman, page 116.

© **International Quilt Festival,** photo of Heather Jones, page 124.

© **Jeffrey Cortland Jones,** photo of Heather Jones, page 125.

© **Shades of Grey Photography,** photo Angela Walters, page 137.

All other photography © the individual quilt maker, except where noted.

A heartfelt thank you to our partners at Janome America whose machines are featured throughout.